Wine
CONFIDENT

This book is dedicated to the three SBs that saw me through:
Sigrid Brenner, Scott Brenner and Sauvignon Blanc.

Wine

CONFIDENT

THERE'S NO WRONG WAY TO ENJOY WINE

Kelli A White

Foreword by Karen MacNeil

Académie du Vin Library

Published 2024 by Académie du Vin Library Ltd
academieduvinlibrary.com
Founders: Steven Spurrier and Simon McMurtrie

Publisher: Hermione Ireland
Editorial Director: Susan Keevil
Art Director: Tim Foster
Design: James Pople
Commissioned photography: © 2024 by Emma K Creative /
emmakcreative.com
Index: Hilary Bird

ISBN: 978-1-917084-49-9

Printed and bound in the EU

Contents

Foreword

When I started to write about wine and, as a result, found myself interviewing winemakers, I came to dread a certain phrase I just knew would be forthcoming...

It didn't matter if my question was something I thought of as simple ('should you let a wine breathe?') or more complex ('do specific flavours come from specific soils?'). The answer was always maddeningly the same:

It depends.

Everything depended on everything else every time. But if everything depended on everything, then how could you ever hope to figure *anything* out? I wanted the comfort of answers, the touchstones of truths. What I got instead was exasperatingly elliptical. Wine 'explanations' were like an infinity loop of variables that kept circling back on themselves until you were dizzy just trying to follow along.

This was why no two winemakers ever gave the same straight answer to any given question.

And as I came to understand much later, it was also why a 'basic' wine book is so hard to write. You can't explain X unless you explain Y which is dependent on Z but only if A and B are true and the weather that year is like C.

Got it?

This is where Kelli White and *Wine Confident* come in. Only the very best wine writers can tackle the tangle of wine's intricacies and pull the yarn apart, laying out the threads just so, making wine knowable and understandable in all its complexity. No mean feat. But it's one that, as you'll see, Kelli has accomplished so well in the pages that follow.

Alas, imparting knowledge that leads to understanding is just part of it. *How* an author does that is everything. In fact, psychologically speaking, I think a good share of wine primers have everything in common with self-help books – that is, they make you feel rotten about yourself, all the while purporting to 'help' you. Not Kelli. She doesn't preach, doesn't dumb stuff down to 'wine baby talk' (her fantastic phrase), doesn't hold herself loftily above her readers. She is right there in the trenches with all the rest of us. Learning. Thinking. Having a great time. Falling in love with wine over and over again.

Wine Confident could be described as a book for wine lovers just starting out. I'd describe it as a book for *smart wine lovers just starting out*. That makes it both fascinating and in a sense, liberating. Reading along, it becomes clear that wine is often counter-intuitive and full of contradictions. It's not that *you're* a dummy; wine *can be* difficult. In her section 'Your Brain on Wine,' for example, Kelli describes why it's so hard to articulate flavour. Music, nongeometric art, grandmothers, chicken soup and foreign films all provide examples that are spot on (you'll just have to read the book!).

I loved Kelli's section on 'Describing Wine to Yourself'. I've often thought that one of wine's greatest challenges is that we *just* drink it. Down the hatch it goes. Nothing wrong with that of course. And yet if you never actually say anything to yourself about a wine, you run the risk that one day, you wake up and realize you've probably tasted hundreds of wines but don't remember much about any of them. It's only by *telling ourselves* something about a wine – using words – that we give ourselves something to remember, something that can be stored in our heads. There are lots of benefits to this. The simple joy of a delicious memory is one. But also, reading wine lists and buying wines get a lot easier once you have a memory bank of wines and their flavours.

I first met Kelli when she was the sommelier at a top Napa Valley restaurant about a decade ago. I'm sure she could talk 'somm talk' just like scores of other sommeliers. But she didn't. She knew that insider wine speak can backfire and make wine drinkers feel somehow inadequate. And so on the pages that follow, she asks us to think about wine using a 'metaphorical world' that makes sense to us – whatever metaphorical world that is.

And she's so right. I remember I once had a 'student' (he was about 50 years old) who was a famous architect. He was part of a small group for whom I gave private wine classes. He rarely gave his opinion of any of the wines we tasted. But one day, I asked him directly what he thought about a certain Bordeaux we were tasting. He got a faraway look in his eyes and said: 'This Bordeaux is the cathedral at Chartres… the flying buttresses… the kaleidoscope of stained glass…' and on and on he went, giving a stunning description. This man wasn't tasting chocolate or cherries in wine. He was *seeing* every wine as a building! We were tasting a majestic, beautifully structured Bordeaux. It made perfect sense.

In the end, there is so much wisdom in *Wine Confident*. And, also, so much beauty and magic. Books like this one are rare. There are practical answers herein, yes. But there is also poetry, for wine has a gravitational ability to captivate us, to move us, to make us feel.

Kelli White has captured it all.

Karen MacNeil, Napa Valley, June 2024

Introduction

My goals in writing this book are simple. To help more people unlock their passion for wine, to deepen their understanding and to increase their confidence.

That last part is especially important. Having been born into a non-wine-drinking family, I am keenly aware of how the industry does a great job at removing some of the joy and enthusiasm that wine can inspire, only to replace it with fear and anxiety. Some stay away from wine because they don't like it. Fair enough. But others steer clear because they are afraid. Afraid to make the wrong decision, afraid to look ignorant, afraid to appear unsophisticated. And that breaks my heart.

What is the origin of this fear?

For both better and worse, wine has an upper-class reputation. The same panic that descends when facing a table-scape loaded with increasingly minute cutlery can strike when leafing through a wine list. Selecting the wrong wine, like reaching for the wrong fork, might seem like an unrecoverable faux pas. A mistake that will leave you humiliated, judged and exposed as an uneducated outsider. (The good news here is that there is no such thing as a 'wrong wine', but more on that later.)

Of course, not everyone feels this same economic or class pressure. They may simply avoid wine because they find the subject overwhelming and don't know where to begin. This is very understandable. The same elements that make wine thrilling – its breadth of regions, varieties and vintages; its ever-changing nature; the many languages of the labels; the rituals that surround its enjoyment – can also make it intimidating.

Which is hopefully where this book comes in handy. In the following pages, I will endeavour to explain wine's fundamentals and its greater mysteries in a friendly, unpretentious and non-condescending way.

This book will go over the basics of wine tasting and service. It will offer tools to help you understand and explain your preferences. It will break down some of the major concepts in wine as well as the inner workings of the wine industry. And most importantly, it will help you select and appreciate wine with confidence!

What this book will not do is detail the hundreds of grape varieties and wine regions found around the world. Those seeking that level of information will have to look elsewhere. The good news is that there are countless resources in that department – some of mine are detailed at the back of *Wine Confident* under Further Reading (page 247).

But what about igniting someone's passion, one of the previously stated goals of this book? To my mind, that's simply a matter of finding a way in.

There are countless points of entry. Are you a history buff? Wine has a multi-thousand-year story to plumb. A lover of language, travel? Wine is being made in more countries than ever before and on every continent except Antarctica. A foodie? Wine is a natural companion to food, and the two can interact in unexpected and thrilling ways. A social activist? Wine has a ton to answer for in terms of its colonial origins and racialized labour practices. A gardener or environmentalist? How a vineyard is farmed can be as important as the grape varieties planted. A student of the arts? The look of a wine label plays a surprisingly key role in market position and consumer expectation. Personally, I love wine's academic depth, especially the science-y bits. That was what first captured my imagination.

Because wine touches so many other spheres of interest, there are many ways to engage with the subject. The rabbit holes are endless, and your passion might lead you down any number of them. You may very well look up in 10 years' time with a cellar full of wine made from some obscure grape variety that stole your heart on a trip abroad. Or fermented using some specific practice. Or farmed according to a particular philosophy.

Alternatively, you might decide that the best way to commune with wine is to sit down, grab a glass and take a sip without giving any of the above a second thought.

There's no wrong way to enjoy wine.

Previous page: *the author performs one of her favourite tasks.*
Opposite: *Wine pairs best with family and friends…*

FALLING IN LOVE
(WITH WINE)

I was not raised with wine. My father is one of those rare abstainers who is not a recovered alcoholic, he simply hates feeling altered in any way; we can barely get the man to take a painkiller. My mother is a bit more relaxed on the subject. Her favourite drink was, and remains, vodka with tonic and lemon. My sister prefers beer.

So how did I find my way into wine?

I came to my improbable career via an impractical major. After both a high school and an early college track dedicated to maths and science (neuroscience was the plan), I abruptly changed my focus to art history. Because I had only two years left, I had to commit all my remaining credits towards completing the major. It was a steep learning curve, but I was sure I'd found my real calling this time.

Sadly, the art world was a financial cold bath. In science, even at the undergrad level, there were paid lab positions and grant money galore. Museums, on the other hand, seemed to demand that you work for free – *for years* – before you gained enough experience to work for very little. I realized I would need to supplement my time in the arts with an outside income. And then I walked past a wine store with a 'Help Wanted' sign in the window.

I had nothing in the way of knowledge to offer my employer, but I was young and strong and not too proud to stack boxes or sweep stairs. I was also incredibly academically driven, and I threw myself into the study of wine with a neophyte's zeal, revelling in wine's central position between science and art – my two fields of interest. I read everything I could get my hands on and dedicated far too much of my hourly wage to bottles, purchased at cost, to study at home.

And I hated it.

I hated everything I tried – both wine and spirits. The appeal of alcohol was completely lost on me. But I had committed my summer to this job and so dutifully stuck it out.

My problem was that I was attempting to go from zero to connoisseur. And because the great writers waxed most lyrically about Bordeaux and Scotch, that was where I started. But even with my industry discount, my meagre paycheck didn't stretch very far. And so I routinely assaulted my tender, inexperienced palate with the gruffness and heat of cheap Cabernet and whiskey. It was not unlike introducing someone to coffee with a double espresso. I needed some cream and sugar to ease into things.

Enter Roussanne.

At the conclusion of my 'summer in wine', I treated myself to a moderately fancy dinner at a restaurant just down the street from the shop. I had walked by it every day and the white tablecloths and flickering candles seemed to promise an as-yet-untasted luxurious side to the business I had so casually entered (and now planned to exit). The sommelier – clearly a good one – considered my food order and budget carefully and made a life-changing recommendation: Châteauneuf-du-Pape Blanc.

The wine was superb. It was everything young Bordeaux wasn't – generous and perfumed and inviting and easy to love. The cushioning apricot flavours of Roussanne, the central grape in this wine, were exactly the soft landing I required. Suddenly, I understood what all the fuss was about. And I was hooked.

Today, I drink very little white Rhône. My tastes have evolved to favour acidity and avoid anything too overtly floral. But I won't apologize for my first love.

And like any first love, I think about it often. I hold on to and talk about this memory because it's important to recall that each of us – even the most celebrated expert – was once new to wine.

WHY WINE MATTERS –
AND HOW IT CAN IMPROVE YOUR LIFE

For many, wine is simply an alcoholic beverage interchangeable with cocktails, beer or even hard seltzer. The thing you drink when the bride and groom didn't shell out for the open bar.

And yet, some people dedicate their lives to its study. An enthusiast might spend hours extolling the complexities of a fine burgundy's bouquet. Collectors will dedicate vast sums of money and equally large chunks of time chasing the rarest gems. And piles upon piles of books have been written on the subject: pocket guides, pairing guides, regional deep dives, encyclopedias, atlases, textbooks, even memoirs. And that's not to mention the online resources, articles, podcasts, videos, films, TV shows and festival after festival after festival. You can study its

A good wine can relax your shoulders after a difficult day at work, enhance your meal, or make potty training a bit more bearable. A great wine can elevate your spirit and connect you to a higher aesthetic realm. Both will get you blissfully buzzed.

manufacture in college. Spend your adult life at tasting courses. Chase accreditations the reputational equivalents of PhDs (sort of). Or join the ranks of the thousands of people labouring to grow, make, sell, buy, import, export, pour, pair or flip the stuff.

Beer and spirits enjoy some of the above, but to quote Elaine Chukan Brown in a 2023 Areni Global podcast, wine is different because 'people fall *in love* with wine. Wine has a romance to it'. Now, I have met some very passionate gin enthusiasts, but I've yet to read a poem dedicated to juniper.

That love Brown references is both powerful and transferable. By association, it can make people fall in love with places (as evidenced in wine tourism), with the growing season, and with agriculture. In this particular podcast, Brown was discussing wine's unique position to stoke consumer concern about the environment in a way that few comestible goods can. Because of the emotional responses it can inspire, wine has the same potential to get people to care about the treatment of farmworkers or international immigration policies. Wine can do that; yoghurt cannot.

Wine plays a fundamental role in many religious ceremonies. Artists across years and mediums have famously used it for creative fuel. But it also has more intimate effects, like bringing a family or a group of friends together over a shared meal. Or toasting one of life's milestones such as the birth of a child, the purchase of a house, the union of a marriage. Learning to slow down and appreciate a glass of wine might help you slow down and appreciate life in general (it certainly did for me). Wine can also make the medicine of a difficult conversation easier to swallow. I have a close friend who reconnected with his estranged father over wine. Their shared interest gave him an excuse to reach out after a long silence, and something to talk about while working up to more difficult matters. And I've been to more than one funeral where

a small group went out afterwards to swap stories over a bottle or two.

A good wine can relax your shoulders after a difficult day at work, enhance your meal, or make potty training a bit more bearable. A great wine can elevate your spirit and connect you to a higher aesthetic realm. Both will get you blissfully buzzed.

I would also submit that there's no easier or better gift to give than a bottle of wine. Because taste in wine is so personal, giving someone a bottle of wine you are passionate about is like giving them a little piece of yourself. And though some of us can take down 750 millilitres without assistance, the standard bottle of wine is sized to be shared. By gifting wine, you are inviting the recipient to connect with another person.

And what could be more meaningful than that?

WINE AS LIFELONG STUDY

Every year, the entire world of wine is born again. This is hardly new commentary. And yet it's worth restating.

Not only is there a novel vintage each year but new wineries open while others close. Virgin ground is planted, and old

blocks are torn up. Even the vines that stay untouched in the ground turn one year older, which subtly affects their performance. Wines in bottle age too, perhaps less subtly. The climate changes. The market changes. Prices fluctuate, as do alcohol laws. The wine world expands

(Poland, Alaska) the wine world contracts (corporate consolidation).

We talk about wine being a natural product, but it is also a fundamentally human one, which further complicates the picture. Properties change hands. Technology improves things or moves us backwards, abandoned traditions are reclaimed. Winemakers die, with or without their secrets. Writers, influencers and tastemakers retire or are launched. A new generation comes into wealth.

And we consumers do not stand still, either. Our palates mature. Our fortunes shift. Our health falters.

All of this adds to the dynamics of wine, making it a lifelong study. It is wonderfully impossible to know everything about wine, and anyone who claims to should be regarded with profound suspicion.

I say this not to overwhelm you with all there is to learn, but to free you from feeling as if you must learn it all. You can't! So don't try. Find what interests you and take it as far as you want to go. Don't worry about the rest. You do not need to be an expert in all wine to appreciate a given wine. You only need to be curious.

Drink. Read. Keep an open mind. Don't let anyone shame you about your tastes or the holes in your knowledge. And stay thirsty. That's pretty much all the wine advice worth giving (but please do keep reading the rest of this book).

A NOTE TO MY READERS

Writing this book made me very nervous.

Being an 'intro to wine' book means it will most likely end up in the hands of people who are just beginning their relationship with wine. It's possible that this book could help shape that relationship. Or end it, if they don't like what they find within. This is a big responsibility! And one I do not take lightly.

For those of us who weren't raised with wine, it can seem an impossibly complex and impenetrable field. Which is why those initial interactions are so important. If your first conversation about wine is with someone who oozes jargon and a superior attitude, you may very well run back into the loving arms of a Tequila Sunrise. If, on the other hand, that dialogue is with someone who listens intently and answers thoughtfully, you might be inspired to dig deeper.

I know this because I lived it. More than once, I almost turned away from wine because of the ways in which it was communicated to me.

My wine career began in Boston in the early 2000s. At that time, there were hardly any other women in prominent positions, at least that I could find. Desperate for some camaraderie, I cast about for women and wine groups and found but one. I turned up for the first tasting with high hopes.

'Merlot', the host began, 'is the little black dress of wine. It goes with everything.' This was quickly followed by a series of shoe metaphors. Granted, this was peak *Sex and The City* era but still, the references felt tired, sexist and more than a bit condescending. I left befuddled and never returned.

The above is an example of what I call 'wine baby-talk'. And while it might work for some people, I found it infuriating. Surely, I remember thinking, there must be a way to simplify this subject without dumbing it down quite so much.

The wine industry has a reputation for being overly florid – and rightly so. But I would argue that wine baby-talk does just as much harm. By emphasizing quick rules, easy answers and overly reductive comparisons, we are setting the budding enthusiast up for confusion and disappointment later on.

Furthermore, the premise that wine is rigid, objective and immutable is false! Wine is flexible, subjective and ever-changing. And I think it's okay to lean into that – to gesture towards the infinite – while breaking the subject down into reasonable nibbles.

In my opinion, the words 'never' and 'always' rarely have a place in wine. Neither do rules, because rules divide us into camps: those who know them and those who don't, those who follow them and those who break them. These divisions create unnecessary anxiety and hierarchies. I believe that if we change the way we talk about wine, we can create a better and more welcoming wine world. One that reflects wine the way I see it – personal, playful, profound and delightfully lawless.

So, if in the following pages I ever sound like I'm contradicting myself, it's probably because I am. I call for simplicity but weave in the technical. I herald plain speech but layer it with poetry. And wherever possible, I substitute easy answers for context. I do this because it's the best way I know to communicate wine's enormity.

Having said that, I fully acknowledge that there are many out there specifically seeking shortcuts. To them I say, if this book doesn't do it for you, don't give up! There are as many wine books as there are ways to speak about wine. Go find one that better resonates with you and do it fast.

Great wine is waiting for you.

1

Tasting Wine

When organizing this book, my original thought was to start with the history of wine. But my editor smartly pointed out that we ought to get right to the heart of the matter. Which is drinking it! So, if you haven't already poured yourself a glass, now is the time to do so.

In some ways, tasting wine is the easiest thing in the world. You swirl, sniff, sip and decide whether you like it. And most people's engagement with wine starts and stops right there. The complexity enters when you try to understand *why* you like a particular wine, or to put what you are tasting into words. For reasons I will touch upon later, the latter is actually incredibly difficult.

The good news is that, like any other skill, you can train for it. And training to become a good wine taster is considerably more fun than training for a half marathon. Naturally, some people are more gifted than others. But even a musical prodigy doesn't sit down at the piano and instantly know how to play. First, they must practice.

HOW TO TASTE

Scientific evidence indicates that we rely on all five of our senses when appreciating wine. Smell and taste are the obvious ones, but touch is also incredibly important, as is sight. Even sound plays a role, with the gentle splashing of wine in a glass and the wet glug of a hearty slurp enhancing our enjoyment.

I would argue that our emotional state and the context in which the wine is consumed affects our impression as well. It all adds up to the total experience of a wine and creates a memory that we access when tasting other wines, or that same wine in the future. But I digress.

For now, let's focus on the specific avenues of sensory impression.

SIGHT

It is well known that the look of a bottle influences the perception of wine. We might, for example, be more inclined to find complexity in a bottle with a pencil drawing of a château on its label than one sporting a panda. But the look of the wine itself – the actual liquid – also shapes our impression. If we see that a wine is red, we may only allow ourselves to recognize aromas associated with red wines. This is why certain scientists and hardcore wine geeks utilize opaque tasting glasses, so that they don't start mentally editing their perceptions.

Note the difference in appearance between the two wines. The lighter hue and amber rim on the right might indicate an older vintage.

Though I relish wine's spectrum of gold, pink, red, purple and orange, I spend far less time on a wine's look than on its smell and taste. But there is still information to be gleaned.

WHITE

'White wine' is certainly a misnomer, as I've yet to see a wine that resembles milk. 'White grapes' are also not a thing, as the berries tend to range from green to grey to pink in colour. Why, then, is the resulting wine relatively clear?

The answer is because white wine is made using only the juice of the grapes, not the skins.

If you went into a vineyard just before harvest, picked a Merlot berry and squeezed it, the juice would be clear. Red wine gets its colour from macerating in contact with the skins for weeks or months prior to pressing. With most white wines, the fruit is pressed right away, and the skins are discarded. That said, a little of the skin character inevitably permeates, which is why white wines can often feature green or gold overtones.

When a wine is particularly golden in hue, it generally means one of three things:

- **Oak:** ageing white wine in oak barrels, especially new oak barrels, will often impart a golden colour. The same effect can be seen in whiskey and *añejo* (aged) tequila, both of which start out completely colourless.
- **Age:** white wines deepen in hue as they age, evolving from gold to brown.
- **Sugar:** many dessert wines are dark gold in appearance. This is especially true for wines made from grapes affected by botrytis (like Sauternes, which is also aged in new oak), or from dried grapes, such as Vin Santo. Learn more about these dessert wines on pages 196–200.

ROSÉ

Rosé is almost always made from red grapes, the skins of which are discarded before too much colour can be extracted. The particular shade of pink is often a reflection of how the wine is made (*see* Chapter 7).

Arguably, the most famous style of rosé is from Provence, where the wines tend to be very pale, sometimes barely even pink, leaning more to salmon or 'onion skin' in hue. With these wines, whole clusters of red grapes are crushed, and the juice is left in contact with the skins for a very short time.

Longer time on the skins makes for a darker shade of pink. The grape variety also matters; rosé made from Grenache grapes, which tend to have thin skins, will be lighter than a rosé made from Cabernet Sauvignon, which has very thick skins.

Certain cultures and regions have traditions pertaining to colour, as well. Greek rosé was often neon to dark pink in tone (though that is changing). That is how the older generations tended to prefer it. I once poured a light rosé for a famous Greek winemaker only to have him hand it back with a playful sneer: 'What is this, water?' Conversely, a Provençal winemaker might be suspicious of an overly pink rosé.

Often, especially dark or bright pink rosé is made via the *saignée* method. This is effectively a byproduct of red winemaking, wherein some of the juice is drained from a newly fermenting tank of red wine. This has the dual benefit of creating a second product (rosé) while concentrating the primordial red wine from which it was drawn. This method is commonly employed in regions that focus on powerful reds.

I once poured a light rosé for a famous Greek winemaker only to have him hand it back with a playful sneer: 'What is this, water?'

LEGS

People often ask whether they should consider a wine's 'legs' or 'tears' – the traces a wine makes down the side of a glass after swirling. My answer is almost always 'no'. Legs are effectively meaningless when assessing a wine, but that wasn't always the case.

Historically, when quality wine production was centred around the cooler reaches of northern Europe, ripeness was paramount. In often-chilly continental climates such as Burgundy's, the hottest vintages were considered the best years, and the warmest vineyards were considered the top sites.

For proof of this, consider the three most celebrated vintages of 20th century Bordeaux: 1947, 1961 and 1982. All were unusually hot years that yielded uncharacteristically ripe wines. According to those souls lucky enough to sample them, generally top 1947 Bordeaux were almost port-like in character. Similarly, it's the warmest, south-facing vineyards along the Mosel that carry the most cachet. And over in Barolo, the sites now dubbed as '*crus*' correspond with remarkable precision to where the snow would historically first melt in the springtime.

How does this tie back to legs?

Higher alcohol wines form tears more readily than lower alcohol wines, and they are faster moving, too. And considering a wine's alcohol content has a direct relation to the level of sugar in its grapes at the time of harvest, warmer places tend to make riper wines. If a connoisseur of yore were to swirl their glass and admire its broad legs, they were likely about to enjoy a wine of high ripeness. And considering the long association of ripeness with quality, they might take that as a very good sign.

Today, however, we live in an era not only of climate change, but of changing consumer preferences. There is an increasing emphasis on wines of elegance, transparency, and yes – lower alcohol levels. Indeed, the best sites aren't always the warmest sites anymore. Which means the information gleaned from a wine's legs isn't nearly as meaningful.

ORANGE

Orange wine is effectively white wine that is made as if it were red. More specifically, it is made from white grapes that are left to ferment on their skins, which is why it is often referred to as a 'skin-contact' white. And because 'white' grapes are neither white nor clear, the resulting wines generally take on an orange or amber hue.

Orange wine may seem like a new phenomenon, but it comes from an ancient style of winemaking. Though many regions moved away from it when technological improvements made the production of clear white wine commonplace, there are a handful of places, such as in Georgia and on the Italian/Slovenian border, where the tradition was never abandoned.

RED

As previously discussed, red wine gets its colour when the juice of a grape macerates with its skins. But not all red wines showcase the same colour or intensity. What accounts for this range?

As with rosé, the darkness of the hue is partly dependent on extraction time (two weeks vs two months, for example), but also on grape type. Pinot Noir is notoriously light in colour because its skins are extremely thin. You could macerate a tank of Pinot Noir on its skins for a year, but the wine would remain somewhat light as there is only a finite amount of pigment to extract.

Climate can also play a role in informing a red wine's hue. In a hotter region, the fruit tends to get sweeter; higher sugars then result in higher alcohols, and alcohol is a powerful extractant. This is partly why big reds from hot places tend to be so dark. Conversely, because colour is stabilized by acidity, and colder climates tend to produce more acidic wines, sometimes it is the cooler location that makes the darker wine. For example, Pinot Noir from Burgundy can be considerably darker than a Pinot Noir from a hotter climate, where it can appear almost bleached.

Wine loves its contradictions.

Confused? Read this!

INSIDE TRACK

CLIMATE, ACID, SUGAR AND ALCOHOL

We are going to discuss this all in greater detail later, but it's worth stopping to explain the link between climate and a given wine's characteristics.

Wine is created when yeasts transform the sugars found in grape juice into alcohol. This process is called fermentation and it's central to the business of winemaking.

There is a direct link between the amount of sugar in grapes and the amount of alcohol in the resulting wine. Therefore, riper grapes make for higher alcohol wines. You can increase ripeness by simply waiting longer to harvest (so long as no rainstorms threaten), but climate also plays a role. Put simply, hotter places tend to make sweeter grapes, which tend to make higher alcohol wines.

Acidity is also affected by climate. Have you ever eaten underripe fruit? Chances are it was not only insufficiently sweet, but also unpleasantly tart. As any fruit ripens, sugar levels rise while acidity falls. Ripening happens faster in hotter climates, so not only does fruit get sweeter, but it gets significantly less tart as well.

Check it out for yourself. Choose a grape variety and purchase two examples, one from a hotter place and one from a colder place. Chances are the cool climate version will have less alcohol and taste slightly more acidic.

SMELL

I often tell my students to stop 'tasting' with their mouths and start tasting with their noses. What I'm attempting to communicate with this advice is that, when it comes to flavour, we get most of the information from our sense of smell.

You can test this theory by holding your nostrils shut while taking a sip of wine (you must continue to pinch even after you swallow). Chances are that the wine will taste of very little. You may have already inadvertently played this game if you are among those that temporarily lost their sense of smell during COVID. I did, and during that time, wine was completely off the table, and food became variously textured lumps-of-nothing that I forced myself to chew for survival.

Remarkably, our olfactory system can discern between thousands of different odours. Wine as a category is believed to encompass around 1,000 scents, making it among the most aromatically complex comestibles. It is almost as if our noses were designed to enjoy wine.

Of course, not everyone has the same abilities. According to wine scientist Jamie Goode, around one-fifth of people can't smell rotundone – a chemical compound found in black pepper that is often referenced in wine, specifically cool climate Syrah. Another portion of the population finds that coriander leaves (cilantro) taste like soap. In other words, wine perception is not perfectly universal – which is another reason why describing wine outwards in a meaningful way is so challenging.

When sniffing wine, don't be afraid to get your nose all the way inside the glass.

ORTHONASAL VS RETRONASAL
A WINE SO NICE I SMELLED IT TWICE

Our noses are complex, sensitive organs that sometimes work in mysterious ways.

If I asked you to smell a wine, you would likely sniff it. You would lower your nose towards the opening of the glass and sharply inhale. This conscious, deliberate act delivers the volatile aromatic compounds emanating from the wine to the olfactory bulb behind your sinuses. The receptors on this bulb interact with the aromatic compounds and translate them into electronic signals that are relayed to the brain for interpretation. This is called orthonasal olfaction and, believe it or not, it is fairly straightforward.

There is another smelling act that occurs after we swallow called retronasal olfaction. But we generally aren't aware that this is happening.

Basically, there is a second tranche of aromatic compounds that make their way to the olfactory bulb via a back door at the top of our throats. These compounds may differ in quantity and/or composition to those we sniffed, due to the actions of our mouths: our chewing or swishing agitates them, the heat inside our mouths increases their volatility, and our saliva begins the digestion process, which alters a food or wine's chemical makeup.

This is the reason why professional tasters might sound like they are gargling when assessing a wine. They are deliberately passing air through the liquid in a bid to release more aromatics. They are going retro!

When it comes to flavour, we get most of the information from our sense of smell.

TASTE

Compared to noses, our mouths are simple machines. Though roughly 5,000 tastebuds are scattered across the surface of the tongue, it is only able to detect five distinct tastes: sweet, salt, sour (acid), bitter (tannin) and umami (savoury, like tomatoes or steak). Flavours are obviously far more streamlined than the aromas on offer, which is partly why a wine's taste is often much easier to describe than its smell.

PRO TIP
AROMATIC VS TEXTURAL TASTERS

Do you find yourself responding more to the bouquet or the texture of a wine? If so, you are not alone. I like to linger over the nose of a wine – I love to decipher its aromas – and often need to remind myself to consider the body and texture as well. This is why I was excited when a friend recently commented that, in his experience, people were either aromatic or textural tasters.

This really resonated with me. And while I don't have any scientific evidence to back it up, the more I think about it the truer it seems. Specifically, I have noticed that most of the winemakers I admire are textural tasters. More than once I've listened to a winemaker go on and on about the tannin signature of a wine while I'm only half paying attention because I'm so focused on the aromatics.

I say this to reassure you. If you find yourself repeatedly focusing on one element of wine over another, don't worry. You aren't doing it wrong. Many people have similar inclinations. The important thing is to recognize what team you're on, then train yourself to pay attention to the other side.

That said, our perception of taste is easily influenced. For example, the high acidity of a German Riesling or champagne has been historically softened through the inclusion of residual sugar. If this sounds strange to you, consider lemonade. We add sugar to lemon juice not to make it sweet, but to make it palatable. One taste (acid) balances the other (sweet). Conversely, a high level of tannin can emphasize acidity, making a wine taste sharper than it might otherwise.

SWEET

Sugar in wine is oddly controversial. At the luxury end of the scale, consumer habits are trending dry, as evidenced by the rise of dry German Riesling, non-*dosage* champagnes (champagnes bottled without residual sugar),[1] and the faltering sales of dessert wines. On the opposite, less-premium, end of the market, a high percentage of wines, even red wines, feature some degree of residual sugar. The result of this dichotomy is that a preference for sweeter wines has gained an unsophisticated association.

To me, this is wine snobbery at its worst. Some of the world's greatest wines are sweet, and delicious examples can be found at all price points. And while it's true that many entry-level wines have residual sugar, not everyone 'graduates' to drier styles as their drinking habits mature.

Sweetness is, of course, a relative term. Dessert wines are often overtly sweet, but 'table wines' (aka, non-dessert wines or wines intended to be consumed with a meal) can range from semi-sweet to featuring an almost undetectable kiss of sugar. How will you know how sweet an unopened wine might be? Unfortunately, each region (Germany, Champagne, Alsace, Austria, Madeira, the Finger Lakes, etc) that regularly produces wines across a spectrum

---

1 *dosage* – a mixture of sugar and wine that is added to champagne just prior to bottling to balance its naturally crisp acidity. *See* p191.

of sweetness has its own distinct labelling practices, which can be difficult to interpret. This is where befriending a wine merchant comes in handy! Sometimes, in wine, the best option is to phone a friend.

It's worth noting that sugar isn't the only thing that makes a wine taste sweet. Oak and alcohol can also interact with the sugar receptors on our tongues in such a way that registers as sweet. Think that high alcohol, oaky Chardonnay has sugar in it? It might. But it also might be playing a trick on your tongue.

SOUR/ACID

The amount of sugar left in a wine is largely a function of winemaking, a deliberate stylistic decision made by a producer. But the acidity of a given wine often comes down to grape genetics. And, as with people, certain varieties are born sour.

Grapes known for their high acid include Riesling, Furmint, Pinot Noir, Nebbiolo, Sauvignon Blanc, Albariño, Barbera, Chenin Blanc and Vidal Blanc. Depending on the overall quality and composition of the wine, this elevated acidity may make the wine taste 'sharp', 'refreshing', appear 'elegant', or may even inspire more precious-sounding attributes such as 'energetic' or 'lifted'. If you feel you have a hard time determining whether a wine's acidity is high or low, pay attention to how much your mouth waters. There's a direct relationship between the tartness of a wine and the amount of saliva we produce in response.

Climate will also affect the amount of acidity in a given wine. Wine grapes begin their lives small, hard, tart and green. As the growing season progresses, the berries get bigger and softer, and change colour. During this process, sugar rises while acidity drops.

Sometimes, in wine, the best option is to phone a friend.

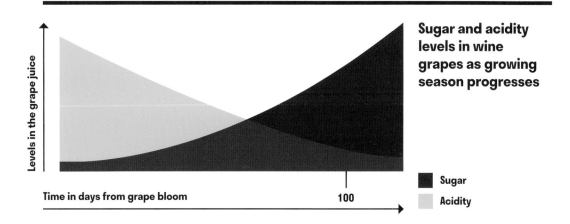

Sugar and acidity levels in wine grapes as growing season progresses

Levels in the grape juice

Time in days from grape bloom · 100

■ Sugar
■ Acidity

In a colder climate, this happens slowly; in a warmer climate, it's more rapid. Because of this, grapes grown in hotter places tend to be lower in natural acidity than those grown on cooler sites. Though a wine's acidic fate is primarily determined by mother nature, a winemaker can influence acid levels by harvesting either earlier (for higher acidity) or later (for lower acidity), within a certain range.

BITTER

Compared to acidity and sweetness, bitterness is not as obvious a wine component, but it still plays a vital role. This taste is commonly associated with tannin, though elevated levels of alcohol can also taste bitter.

Tannins are a tricky subject because they interact with our palate in complex ways. Most of the tannin in wine comes from grape skins. These tannin molecules are fairly large and bind with the proteins in our saliva, creating a sense of dryness or astringency in the mouth. Smaller-grained tannins, such as those found in grape seeds and new oak barrels, are compact enough to interact with receptors on our tastebuds, triggering a sense of bitterness. A little bitterness can add welcome complexity to a wine, but too much can be off-putting. This is why great care is taken during fine winemaking to avoid the crushing of seeds.

Tannins are commonly associated with red wine, but they are present in other styles as well. Some rosés feature a light tickle of tannins, and orange wine can be quite grippy. Certain white wines sport a subtle tannic edge, often referred to as 'phenolic bitterness'. This is observed in white wines that either come from naturally tannic grapes (like Grüner Veltliner and Ribolla Gialla) or have enjoyed some degree of skin contact prior to pressing.

SALTY AND UMAMI

Salty and savoury are qualities most commonly associated with the food we eat, but these tastes play an important role in the enjoyment of wine, too.

Wines contain a host of mineral salts, which can contribute to a sensation of saltiness (generally quite subtle). This area of wine taste is comparatively understudied, but it is thought that certain soil types (chalky, volcanic), proximity to the sea, and/or drought stress might increase the concentration of salt in a wine. Our brains can also trick our palates into believing a wine tastes salty if its bouquet is redolent of salty foods, such as oysters or Parmesan.

Wines often described as salty include Albariños from Rías Baixas (Spain), certain champagnes, Barossa Shiraz (Australia), sherry, madeira and Assyrtiko from Santorini (Greece).

Umami is our most recently discovered taste, with the tastebud receptors identified in 2002. These receptors are triggered by certain amino acids (the building blocks of protein). As with saltiness, the role umami plays in wine is still being explored, but research indicates that red wine has significantly higher levels of amino acids, and therefore is more inclined to taste savoury. It has also been implied that this savoury quality becomes more obvious as a wine ages.

WHAT IS TANNIN?

Tannins are a group of compounds known as polyphenols, which is why the term 'phenolic' gets thrown about in wine discussions. They are found in the skins, seeds, leaves and wood of many plants and were historically used to 'tan' animal hides into leather (hence the name). Tannins are astringent by design, as they are meant to dissuade curious animals or insects from eating a plant before it is ready to be consumed. You have experienced tannins outside a wine context if you've ever eaten a green banana, which completely dries out your mouth. The astringency of overly steeped tea is also due to tannin.

In wine, tannin is often credited with giving a red wine its 'structure'. Certain varieties are more inherently tannic than others. Pinot Noir is known for being light in tannin while Cabernet Sauvignon, Xinomavro and Nebbiolo are notoriously tannin-rich.

This simple chart is a handy reference for understanding red wine tannin levels but it can never be exact. Bottles will vary. A wine's position on this scale will depend on its region, the style preference of the winemaker, the age of the wine and the vintage.

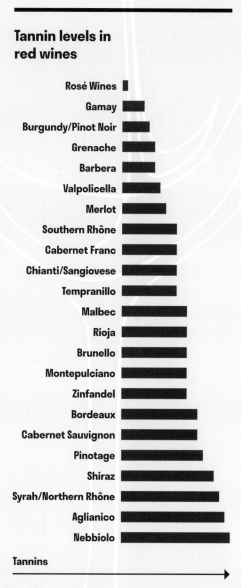

Tannin levels in red wines

Rosé Wines
Gamay
Burgundy/Pinot Noir
Grenache
Barbera
Valpolicella
Merlot
Southern Rhône
Cabernet Franc
Chianti/Sangiovese
Tempranillo
Malbec
Rioja
Brunello
Montepulciano
Zinfandel
Bordeaux
Cabernet Sauvignon
Pinotage
Shiraz
Syrah/Northern Rhône
Aglianico
Nebbiolo

Tannins →

PRO TIP
THE FINISH

What is a wine's finish, how do you measure it, and is it different from length?

Though the terms 'finish' and 'length' are used somewhat interchangeably, length is just one component of a wine's finish. Properly speaking, finish is the final flavour and textural impression of a wine, while length is the amount of time that those flavours linger on the palate. Some professional tasters measure and record the length in seconds – ideally using a quaint stopwatch – but this is less common now than it was a generation ago.

A long finish is generally associated with high quality but it's unclear why the two are linked. Common thought is that great wines are complex, layered, balanced and have considerable detail to their flavour (I hesitate to say 'full-

A NOTE ABOUT THE TONGUE MAP

Sometime in my early education, I was presented with a tongue map and received it as fact. You are probably familiar with what I am referring to – a kind of butcher's diagram of the human tongue, with 'sweetness' localized to the tip, 'saltiness' at the sides, etc. Please erase it from your mind.

The tongue map lobby has been remarkably effective in propagating this school of thinking, but the theory was debunked long ago. It turns out that our taste receptors are scattered more or less evenly across the tongue.

So please stop worrying about where wine lands on your palate when you sip it...

flavoured' lest that disadvantage subtle wines like red burgundy) and that those characteristics take longer to unfold and resolve.

Still confused? Taste an inexpensive Pinot Grigio* next to a fine white burgundy. Most likely, the burgundy will linger far longer on your palate.

Another analogy to help explain a wine's length, and how this differs from other criteria in the tasting experience, is with the piano. When you strike a key to produce a note, there's the attack (initial impression of the wine) followed by the sustain (the finish). The number of seconds you can still hear the note as it fades is the length.

* No disrespect to Pinot Grigio (also known as Pinot Gris), which can make some wonderful and truly world class wines, but the overwhelming popularity of the grape invites industrialization, so it's relatively easy to find tragically benign versions in most markets.

TOUCH (AKA TEXTURE)

Touch is perhaps the most underappreciated of all the senses used in wine. This is likely because we don't typically think of 'touching' things with the inside of our mouths. Nonetheless, touch is the primary mechanism by which we assess a wine's texture.

Touch tells us how dense and/or drying a wine's tannins are, whether it has bubbles, its palate weight and temperature. These sensations are critical to wine's enjoyment, and some of wine's most-commonly heard descriptors, such as 'smooth' or 'bold', relate to texture.

Of all the qualities listed above, palate weight is perhaps the most mysterious. The most commonly cited metaphor involves milk. All milk is milky. And yet there is a clear difference in texture between skimmed one percent, two percent, whole milk and cream. Try using this scale to calibrate and compare the wines you taste, and the concept of 'palate weight' will hopefully begin to make sense. For example, I typically find that Sauvignon Blanc is often in the one percent range while Chardonnay will vary from two to whole.

What makes one wine fleshier than another? There are many possibilities, but chief among them are alcohol, sweetness, genetics and winemaking techniques.

Both residual sugar and high levels of alcohol will increase the density of a wine (though, as previously discussed, elevated acidity might alter our perception here). The grape in question will also play a role, as some varieties are simply more substantial. Pinot Gris/Grigio, for example, is notoriously viscous, while Nebbiolo is often lean. The way a wine is made is also important, with more 'extractive' techniques such as lees-stirring, pumpovers/punchdowns, and extended maceration resulting in a richer, denser wine (for an explanation of these terms, *see* chapter 7). It has also been shown that wines made in an oxidative style (ie, aged in oak, where oxygen is encouraged to be part of the process, versus stainless steel, where oxygen is excluded) tend to be creamier in feel.

FLAVOUR AND THE BRAIN

If you're used to thinking things along the lines of, 'this dry Riesling tastes like lemons', you might find the above confusing. From a technical perspective, the wine *tastes* sour and it *smells* citrusy. These two senses are combined in your brain along with texture (lean) and sight (white) to form an overall impression of the wine's flavour (lemon).

The fact that flavour is created in the brain and not on the tongue may come as a surprise. Traditionally, if I wanted to know the flavour of something, such as an ice cream, I would lick it. Lick that same scoop with a stuffed-up nose and the flavour almost disappears. So why do we persist in thinking we taste with just our mouths?

Because our brains want it that way.

According to Dr Jamie Goode's book, *The Science of Wine* (2020), flavour – what we colloquially describe as 'taste' – is 'localized to the mouth by the sense of touch' because 'this is where any response to the food or drink, such as swallowing it or spitting it out, will need to take place'. In other words, linking the sensory assessment of food and drink to our mouths is in the interest of our own self-preservation. If we chew a piece of rotten food, we can eject it instinctively without too much internal debate. A similar impulse takes hold when sipping our uncle's bathtub gin.

My hope is that digging into the technical aspects of flavour and the senses is exciting, rather than overwhelming. For me, it led to a whole new level of enjoyment. Understanding that flavour is so much more than 'taste' taught me that a more holistic, or meditative approach to wine appreciation was in order. In other words, don't just focus on the nose or the palate – open all your senses to the experience. Your tasting skills will be the better for it.

THE MECHANICS OF TASTING

It's all well and good to examine the science behind wine appreciation, but what if you don't know how to hold a wine glass. Where do you begin?

HOLDING THE WINE GLASS

Wine glasses are typically held by the stem for reasons both practical and aesthetic. If you have taken care to serve your wine at the proper temperature, holding it by the stem stops your hand from warming the wine. It also prevents the accumulation of fingerprints on the glass. My husband, our resident glass washer, is always harping on about this.

Conversely, holding a glass by the bowl is appropriate if the wine you have been served is too cold and you need to warm it. This may also be the only option if you are drinking wine out of a stemless glass or tumbler.

There's no problem holding a wine glass at its base. I don't do it simply because I have never quite figured out how to put it down one-handed from that position (I am usually holding food in the other hand).

Holding glasses by their stems (as we all are here) allows the wine to remain a cool complement to most dishes. Not overthinking wine pairings sets you free to experiment. My favourite dinner parties are pot lucks with a mixed assortment of wines.

SWIRL

Because they are invisible, we sometimes forget that aromas are molecules – with different sizes, weight and volatility – that need to physically rise out of the wine and reach our noses. This is where swirling comes in handy.

If you are not used to swirling, it's best to practice with the base flat on a table and not too much wine in the glass. Once you get the hang of that, practice swirling in the air. Eventually, it will become an almost subconscious reflex. I once swirled my beer in a dive bar, which is not a great way to impress the locals.

If you really want to geek out, train yourself to smell your wine in three phases – before swirling, just after swirling, and again when the glass is empty. The difference in aromas may be very subtle, but there are distinctions.

SNIFF

This is a fairly straightforward act but refer to page 27 for a breakdown of orthonasal vs retronasal olfaction.

SIP

Sipping is probably the element of wine tasting in which professionals differ most starkly from consumers. If you've been to a formal tasting, you might have witnessed the following: a very serious person solemnly sips their wine, swishes it about their mouths, opens their lips slightly and appears to gargle and then spits or swallows in silent contemplation.

The scene above may seem beyond pretention, but there is some method to this wine lover's madness. Though I previously stated that the tongue map is best ignored, there is still some sensory advantage to making sure the wine hits all parts of your mouth. Plus, the act of swishing warms and agitates the wine, which adds another dimension to the flavour. That gargling, as already discussed, is our pretend connoisseur's attempt to aerate the wine

Swirling your wine in the glass can enhance a wine's aromatics.

in their mouth. It sends another wave of aromas back up behind the soft palate and into the nasal cavity, enriching appreciation.

If you've never tasted wine in this way, I recommend practicing at home, as initial attempts tend to come with a high risk of dribbling. Having said that, please feel free to skip the above and simply sip your wine as you would any other beverage. It will still taste great!

SPIT

Spitting is an essential act for wine professionals; it's the only way to taste a volume of wines without becoming ludicrously intoxicated. Most consumers would probably never consider spitting out a wine unless it was truly bad or had a bug in it, but it can be a useful skill. Should you ever find yourself in a situation, such as a wine fair or winery visit, where there is more on offer than you would typically consume, try spitting. You get the same flavour and improved sensory perception but without all the pesky ex-texting.

FLAWS

It's hard enough to sort through the world of wine and determine your preferences without having to contend with flaws. But unfortunately, flawed wines are all too real a concern. There are many things that can go wrong with a bottle of wine and very few are visible from the outside. Detecting them requires a bit of palate training.

This is where professional assistance is essential. If you are at a restaurant and concerned your wine may be flawed, ask a sommelier, manager, waiter or bartender with a working knowledge of wine to taste it. Assuming they can confirm the wine is indeed damaged, most restaurants will exchange it without fuss. When it comes to retail, the best strategy is to bring the bottle back – unfinished – as soon as you can. Your chance of talking a retailer into a refund increases if you can return the wine while still relatively fresh, so that the flaw might be detectable. But do bear in mind that precise policies on this point vary from business to business.

It is also important to note that flaws exist on a spectrum. A wine can be very oxidized or lightly oxidized; extremely bretty or barely bretty[1]. Whether it registers as pleasant or unpleasant depends on the preference of the drinker. As an example, I love reduction but am sensitive to volatile acidity (VA). A good friend of mine who also happens to be a Master Sommelier loves VA and also enjoys rancio-style wines (deliberately oxidized). A little tolerance will serve you well as you explore the wide and sometimes wild world of wine.

CORK TAINT

If I were in charge, one of the first things about wine that I would change is the term 'corked'. It is very misleading. I can't tell you how many times I've had a guest think that being 'corked' just meant that a wine was bottled under cork. And then they're confused as to why that's a bad thing. It isn't. 'Corked' is just a short-hand way of a saying a wine has 'cork taint' – aka TCA (2,4,6-trichloroanisole) or a related compound.

Wine corks are harvested from the bark of the cork oak tree, which grows most famously in Portugal. TCA forms in the bark and leeches into the wine via its cork, which is why wines bottled under screw cap are effectively safe from this specific taint.

There are many ways to describe cork taint's particular mustiness. Some say wet dog, others rotting geranium, still others say grandma's basement or wet newspapers.

---

1 hold tight… explanations for 'bretty' and the next handful of wine terms will follow on pages 44–45.

I THINK THIS WINE IS CORKED BUT THE SOMMELIER DOESN'T AGREE... NOW WHAT?

This is a very tricky situation to navigate, and I have been on both sides.

One time, a small group of female wine professionals and I went out to dinner and our wine was corked. We all agreed, and I flagged down the waiter and asked for a replacement bottle. He rolled his eyes dramatically and removed the glasses with exaggerated reluctance. When the second, unblemished bottle arrived, I invited him to taste the two side by side (he didn't taste either before serving, and I really wish he had – it would have saved everyone a lot of time). He declined, saying: 'I don't need to, I'm sure both bottles are fine. Wines vary! This is something you will learn.' You can imagine my blood pressure.

This is an extreme example, but even more benign interactions along these lines can leave a guest feeling frustrated and upset. It is my belief that a restaurant should not force a guest to pay for a bottle they believe to be damaged. If, on the other hand, the consumer simply doesn't like a particular wine and wants to send it back, that's harder to justify. A restaurant can likely get its money back from a distributor if a wine is, in fact, flawed. If a restaurant must swallow the cost of multiple bottles simply because the guests are unhappy, that can dramatically affect its bottom line. This is one of the many reasons why careful listening on the part of the sommelier, and clear communication on the part of the guest, is paramount.

What would I do when a guest believed a bottle was flawed and I did not? First, I would always take it off the bill. Then I would encourage them to try a different wine instead, rather than fetch another bottle of the first (in case the issue was that they simply didn't like it). Finally, I would attempt to recoup the cost of the bottle by offering it as a special glass pour that evening. If I was unable to sell the wine through, the rest would be used as staff training at the end of the night.

A sommelier's job is to balance guest happiness with the financial health of the restaurant. Ideally without sacrificing one to the other.

Cork taint can make a wine taste muted or truncate its finish. But its primary characteristic is its funk. There are many ways to describe cork taint's particular mustiness. Some say wet dog, others rotting geranium, still others say grandma's basement or wet newspapers. Unfortunately, a few of these descriptors are redolent of aromas commonly found in aged wine, such as 'library' or 'cigar box'. This is why the uninitiated might think a wine is corked when it simply smells a bit old.

However you describe it, TCA gives off a very specific odour that, once properly learned, is hard to mistake for anything else. Identifying cork taint is important because if you don't know how to recognize it and are served a corked bottle, you might just think you don't like that wine. Which is unfair to the hardworking people who made it.

What's the best way to familiarize yourself with TCA's distinctive stink? Ask your favourite wine professional if they have any corked bottles around. If you don't feel like waiting for the flawed stars to align, however, you can always purchase a Le Nez Du Vin fault kit which will help you detect any problems.

Cork taint is the exception to my previously espoused 'spectrum of flaws' theory. Even a slight whiff of it ruins a wine for me. For years, I believed this was a universal truth among wine professionals until one evening, working the floor in Napa Valley, I opened a bottle that I suspected might be corked but wasn't quite sure. Because the wine was very rare, and because the guest was a prominent winemaker, I asked for his opinion. He insisted it was sound and proceeded to drink it with gusto. Upon leaving, he admitted that the wine was, in fact, slightly corked. Horrified, I attempted to remove it from the tab, but he wouldn't hear of it. 'The wine was still so enjoyable,' he assured me: 'Like a beautiful painting with a very small tear.' Though I appreciated his aesthetic flexibility, I had to respectfully disagree. To my palate, cork taint, even in small amounts, is a wine killer.

PRO TIP
TIPS FOR DETECTING CORK TAINT

1 Go with your gut instinct. Have you ever smelled a wine, thought it was corked, only to go in for a deeper sniff and start second-guessing yourself? This isn't cork taint being sneaky, this is your brain messing with you. In some senses, that first sniff of wine is the most potent. As the brain gets used to what's in front of it, it begins shuttling scents to the background. This is not unlike how your house smells virtually odourless to you but has a definite scent to visitors. In tracking my own experiences, anytime I instinctively thought a wine was corked, I was usually right.

2 When in doubt, decant. My entire sommelier career was spent at restaurants dedicated to older vintages. Every so often a bottle would display musty notes upon opening that were worryingly similar to cork taint. The fastest way to find out whether a wine was corked or just musty was to decant it. Funk blows off, cork taint only gets worse with air.

BRETTANOMYCES

It is arguable as to whether brettanomyces is a flaw. Many people, such as myself, enjoy a touch of 'brett' in their wines. When in balance with the rest of the wine, it can present as leather or 'barnyard' (that's fancy wine-speak for manure) or impart a pleasant smoky aroma. When out of whack it can be redolent of Band-Aids or aspirin.

What is Brettanomyces? It is a yeast, but not the one typically used in wine fermentations.

During fermentation, yeasts convert grape sugar into alcohol. The byproducts of this reaction are heat, carbon dioxide and a selection of aromatic compounds. In wine, the dominant yeast is called Saccharomyces. The scents it produces have been associated with wine for so long that it is more or less considered it to be aromatically neutral.

There are other non-Saccharomyces yeast strains that consume sugar – some good, some bad. The worst of these are spoilage yeasts that hasten a wine's transformation to vinegar. Others are naturally present in vineyards, and some winemakers encourage their participation during fermentation. It is thought that this use of ambient (as opposed to inoculated) yeast produces a wine that is both more authentic to its origin and aromatically complex. Whether Brettanomyces is a spoilage yeast or an agent of complexity is a matter of intense debate among wine lovers.

Brettanomyces is a particularly hardy yeast and, in addition to vineyards, can 'infect' whole barrels, wineries, even wine regions. Getting rid of brett requires intense hygiene protocols and perpetual vigilance. That said, some wineries are so enamoured of their strains that they embrace it as part of their house style.

> **Many people, such as myself, enjoy a touch of 'brett' in their wines.**

OTHER FLAWS

Cork taint and Brettanomyces are just the tip of the iceberg. The remaining flaws can be effectively divided into qualities present in the wine at the time of bottling (mousiness, smoke taint, volatile acidity) and those picked up after the wine is in bottle (heat damage, light damage, oxidation), which are typically the result of poor storage conditions.

The following is a brief guide to these more minor flaws, what causes them, and what they taste like.

Oxidation

Oxidation occurs when – plot twist – a wine is exposed to excessive oxygen. This sometimes happens during the winemaking process but is more commonly due to cork failure. Oxidized wines taste nutty (especially if white), tired and often volatile. An oxidized wine will typically decline rather quickly. Having said that, *deliberately* oxidized wines, such as tawny port, can be quite long-lived.

Heat damage

A wine that has experienced heat damage might taste cooked, tired, lack fruit or appear oxidized. It, too, will experience a truncated lifespan. Often, a wine that has been exposed to heat will exhibit a protruding cork or show 'signs of seepage', which is auction-house-speak for ooze. Heat causes the liquid in the bottle to expand, which can push against or saturate the cork.

Light damage

A light damaged or 'light struck' wine will either prematurely oxidize or develop stinky, sulphury aromas reminiscent of garlic or cabbage. This is a good reminder to store your wines in a dark corner and never select a bottle from the display window of a wine shop.

Reduction

Like brett, reduction can be quite pleasant in low doses. Indeed, it is currently trendy to produce wines, especially Chardonnay, in a deliberately reductive style. When deftly managed, the result is a flinty or stony aromatic overtone. When flubbed, an overly reductive wine can get quite stinky. If your wine is slightly reduced and you find it displeasing, decant it. Sometimes a little air will blow off that flinty smell.

Volatile acidity

A little volatile acidity can give a wine 'lift' and enhance its aromatic profile. Too much volatile acidity smells like nail polish remover. VA is generated by bacteria that, if left unchecked, will transform your wine into vinegar.

Smoke taint

While smokiness is often considered a positive attribute, smoke taint is something else altogether. One of the unfortunate consequences of the increasing prevalence of wildfires is that an affected region's wines might develop smoke taint.

This may sound ominous but the conditions for the development of smoke taint are quite specific. First, the fire must occur in close proximity to the vineyard; a smoky sky alone is insufficient to damage fruit. Secondly, smoke can only infect the grapes if they are ripe and still on the vine. Unripe fruit seems largely immune to the ill-effects of smoke, as is an actively fermenting tank.

Smoke taint can be subtle but often increases with time in the bottle. The worst examples display a bitter, almost ashy quality on the finish.

Mousiness

This extremely unfortunate flaw is mostly confined to wines that are produced with low or no added sulphites, a natural preservative used to stabilize wines and protect them from oxidation and bacterial infections. Bacterial action results in a particularly nasty aroma redolent of a dead mouse or mouse cage (it is unlocked by saliva, so is only detected retronasally, after you've already swallowed). Luckily for them, about a third of the population can't detect this compound.

2

Talking Wine

'What do you taste in this wine?'

I recently had a client, a new but curious wine drinker, come to me in a panic. A tasting room attendant had posed to her that exact query and she froze. Unable to pick out specific aromas such as blackberry or clove, she descended into insecurity. She became convinced that something was wrong with her palate, or that she couldn't appreciate wine at the same level as other people. Needless to say, the winery also lost a potential sale.

To the uninitiated, 'what do you taste?' is a dreaded question. And yet, we ask it all the time.

Picking specific aromas or flavours out of a glass of wine is an extremely difficult act. And in my opinion, the more wine writers and sommeliers pretend that this is not only intuitive but the best way to communicate about wine, the more people we will alienate. So why is it so hard, and how can we make it easy?

YOUR BRAIN ON WINE

Why is it so hard to articulate a wine's flavour? According to author, neuroscientist and Yale professor Gordon M Shepherd, it has to do with the way our brains are wired.

In his book, *Neurogastronomy – How the Brain Creates Flavor and Why it Matters* (2013), Shepherd investigates the relationship between language and smell – the foundation of flavour – and makes several suggestions as to why their union might be fraught. The classic trope among scientists is that the speech centres of the brain are physically quite far from our smell-processing area, resulting in a weakened connection. But Shepherd contends that the issue is more that our brain processes smells as patterns, similar to the way in which we process faces.

To illustrate his point, he calls upon Grandma. 'Humans are in fact very good at recognizing faces,' he explains. 'The classical illustration of this is that in a room full of grandmothers, you can readily identify your own grandmother. Yet if you are asked to describe your grandmother's face to someone else, it is very difficult; we lack the vocabulary… to specify how this pattern recognition is carried out. But we do it unerringly.' He goes on to say that we encounter the same linguistic block when attempting to articulate other abstract inputs such as music, nongeometric art and wine.

Wine is especially challenging because a single glass can contain several hundred aromatic compounds. And, according to

> **Wine is especially challenging because a single glass can contain several hundred aromatic compounds.**

Shepherd, smell is synthetic, not analytic, which means that 'a mixture of several smells makes a new unified smell'. A good example of this is the way that chicken soup smells like chicken soup, rather than chicken + carrot + onion + parsley + broth + bay leaf. That's not to say it isn't possible to smell a bowl of chicken soup and pick out the carrot notes, but it is significantly harder to tease out the ingredients than it is to recognize the whole.

Breaking a wine down into its component aromas is even more challenging, in part because they are invisible (ie, no chunks of celery floating in your Chianti) but also, Shepherd alludes, because smell is processed almost exclusively on the right side of the brain. This is known to be the less logical and more creative half of our heads, which might explain the longstanding link between wine and poetry.

But Shepherd's final and perhaps most important point is that our sense of smell is intricately bound with the memory and emotion centres of our brains. Memory (I remember this) and emotion (it was good) were critical to early man's sense of smell, which was used to help differentiate food from poison and enemy from friend. Even today, it is almost impossible to separate flavour from emotion, especially when you consider that preference is an emotion. And whether it's a wisp of perfume, an old shirt, or a tea-soaked madeleine, scents are notorious for conjuring memories in profoundly visceral ways.

MUSIC AND WINE

A great bottle of wine can enhance one's mood. But a great mood can also enhance a wine. Or at least that's what certain wineries and restaurants are banking on.

I recently had the pleasure of tasting at a winery that was busily preparing for the imminent arrival of a renowned critic. The scores this critic might award would have a profound financial impact on this winery and tensions were high. How were the winery principles getting ready? By creating a special playlist featuring the critic's favourite songs.

It's true. The critic in question was a notorious music lover and the thinking was that his preferred music playing subtly in the background might subconsciously encourage a more favourable impression of the wines. This is the same reason many restaurants spend thousands on professionally curated playlists. When it comes to taste, it is very difficult to separate the psychological from the physical.

What does all this mean for the budding wine enthusiast?

I'm not saying it's pointless to try and describe wine. On the contrary, articulating what a wine tastes like and how much you enjoy it are essential parts of connoisseurship. What I'm trying to communicate is that if it seems hard at first, that's because it is.

I also hope to encourage wine lovers to not simply focus on the information coming out of the glass. Relaxing into the total experience of a wine will enhance your appreciation. Let those memories and emotions in! And pay attention to the context in which you are enjoying your wine – your state of mind, the time of day, the way the light falls across your partner's face. These will become part of the new memory layer your brain will knit into this wine; yours to revisit the next time you pour yourself a glass.

GLASS FULL OF METAPHORS

Wine's ability to smell like anything other than its base material is one of its most compelling aspects. Fermented wine grapes can evoke anything from roses to roasted coffee to rain falling on rocks.

This extraordinary feature leads to considerable misunderstanding. My husband makes a small amount of wine each year and bottling is always the most stressful part. One year, I happened to catch up on the phone with a friend just beforehand and was complaining about the day ahead. 'What's so stressful?' she enquired. 'Haven't you already added all the stuff?' 'What stuff, sulphur?' I asked. 'No,' she replied, 'you know, the lemon, the leather...'

I was floored. At this point, I had been in the wine industry for over 15 years and my close friend thought that winemakers literally add cassis to their Cabernet. If this exchange had happened on a reality television programme, I would have been told to pack up my corkscrew and leave.

In addition to underscoring my complete failure as a wine educator, this exchange revealed for me how confused many people are about wine's fundamentals. It was also a good reminder not to assume a certain level of understanding in the people around me, and to be clearer in my communications.

So let me be clear. While wine might share the same compounds as familiar foodstuffs (isoamyl acetate, for example, which gives bananas their characteristic odour, is often found in wine), it is produced exclusively of grapes, with minor aromatic contributions from yeast and barrel.

Wine conjures many things it does not contain. Or as my colleague Sarah Bray once brilliantly put it, what you are tasting is metaphors.

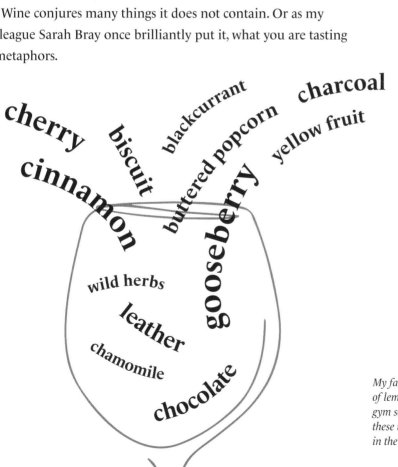

My favourite Chablis smells of lemon curd, Parmesan and gym socks. Thank goodness these things aren't literally in the wine.

DESCRIBING WINE TO YOURSELF

Before you can effectively describe wine outwards, you must be able to explain it to yourself. This is critical. You need to calibrate your palate so that you have an internal reference bank against which to measure any new wines that come your way.

Calibrating your palate takes a little time but it's well worth the effort. And by 'effort' I mean tasting a bunch of wines and paying attention to your observations. There are two major steps to take in this pursuit.

STEP ONE: SAMPLE BROADLY

It's important to expose yourself to a range of wines, even if you revert right back to drinking the same old thing. Exposure builds context, and it's almost impossible to have an effective conversation about wine without at least some context.

Not only should you attempt to taste wines from as many different regions and grape varieties as possible, you also ought to focus on specific wine attributes such as acidity, tannin, alcohol level, sweetness and aromatic intensity, among others. Alcohol content is perhaps the easiest to gauge; it's written on the label, after all. For the others, ask a knowledgeable retailer or sommelier to provide recommendations. I promise that the first time you taste a Gewürztraminer (heady and floral) next to a Semillon (subdued), you will understand the full range of wine's aromatic intensity.

YOUR PALATE, YOUR VOICE

When first writing about wine, I worked within what I believed to be the established template. I wrote tasting notes that addressed first the colour, then the bouquet, then the texture of a wine. My inventories of aromatic descriptors were as romantic as a grocery list and half as useful. I postured, I pontificated. Many things burst from the glass.

One day I found myself describing a wine as 'voluptuous and sexy' and I stopped. What the hell was I talking about? As a straight woman, voluptuous wasn't necessarily a sexy quality to me. And what did sex appeal have to do with anything, anyway?

I realized I had been describing wine using someone else's words. I had subconsciously assumed the perspective of the (historically) older white men that had dominated wine criticism for so long because that was the only point of view available to me. I had neither the confidence nor the permission I thought I needed to find my own voice. And using someone else's language to write about wine meant I had also been using someone else's palate to assess it.

Learning to trust my own judgement, to examine what truly excited me about a given wine, and to express that in my own way, was life changing. I stopped worrying about saying the right thing and ordering the right thing. The more wine-confident I became, the more I realized that the opinion that mattered most was my own. And suddenly everything got a lot more fun.

The easiest way to sample a number of different wines is either by buying a mixed case at your local retailer, or ordering wine by-the-glass at restaurants. Ideally, you'd taste multiple wines at the same time. Comparing two or more wines to each other is the fastest and best way to build context, as opposed to trying them one at a time. If this feels like a financial burden, you can always share the load by starting a tasting group. Finding even just one friend with an interest in wine can cut your expenses in half.

Here is an example of why context is essential to communication.

Syrah is notoriously hard to sell to Americans; as a result, Americans have limited exposure to the variety. When I was working as a sommelier in Napa Valley and would suggest a Syrah, guests would either respond with 'No thanks, I'm not looking for anything that heavy' or 'No thanks, I'm not looking for anything that light'.

Even though Syrah can boast a remarkable range of expressions, I was always flummoxed by the strength and surety of these responses. Today, I wonder if those consumers lacked the context to appropriately describe Syrah because they had only exposed themselves to a limited selection of wines. To a dedicated Cabernet drinker, Syrah might indeed seem rather light. Meanwhile, a Pinot Noir enthusiast might find Syrah far too intense.

I'm making a lot of assumptions about these guests and their drinking habits. But the point is, without the context to properly describe Syrah to yourself, there is no hope of explaining to someone else why you may or may not want a bottle.

STEP TWO: FIND A MEANINGFUL METAPHOR

Wine is a vague, complex beverage that is neurologically challenging to describe. Reaching for a metaphor can sometimes be the best way to articulate it to yourself. Forget for a minute the way other people talk about wine. Find your own language and frames of reference.

Here is what I mean.

My colleague Sarah once hosted a couple for a blind tasting class. It began by tasting through a range of wines – their labels covered so the contents had to be guessed at. They discussed the dominant aromas and textures and what they might signify (high acidity = cool climate, and so forth). The wife was not amused. She didn't see how Sauvignon Blanc and Chardonnay were different – they both tasted like white wine to her. She found the concept of 'palate weight' ridiculous and certainly didn't want to talk about gooseberries!

Later in the conversation it came out that she was a skier and Sarah made one last attempt to engage her in the tasting. The Sauvignon Blanc with its vibrant acidity and high-toned aromatics, she explained, was like skiing moguls – it was energetic, it had movement. Whereas the broad, creamy Chardonnay was like cruising in deep powder. The woman begrudgingly revisited the wines and her eyes lit up. Suddenly, she got it. She had found a way in.

I had a similar experience with an interior designer. She expressed insecurity in her tasting abilities but after a little conversation it was clear that she had a very good palate. She tended to prefer big reds but was quite discriminating when it came to tannic structure. Given her profession, she likened a wine's texture to fabric. Whether it was tweed, linen or jersey cotton, she had a reference point for every imaginable mouthfeel. She was embarrassed by her system because it didn't conform to how most people talked about wine, but I reassured her that she was on the right track.

Finding your own way of describing wine, one that makes consistent sense to you, is the best first step.

> **She likened a wine's texture to fabric. Whether it was tweed, linen or jersey cotton, she had a reference point for every imaginable mouthfeel.**

DESCRIBING WINE TO OTHERS

O k. You've done the work, sampled a bunch of different bottles, and feel that you have at least a decent grasp of the range of wines available. It's time to start talking about what you are tasting.

Where to begin?

START WITH TASTE AND TEXTURE

As previously discussed, there are hundreds of different aromatic compounds in wine but only five tastes: sweet, sour, bitter, salt and umami. Because of this, it is considerably easier to focus on taste. Texture – how dry, fleshy, lean or even alcoholic – is also a good place from which to commence.

This strategy works because taste and texture seem to drive preference, therefore people are more in tune with them (or vice versa). I have had countless guests tell me that they don't want anything too tannic, too acidic, too alcoholic or too sweet. But I've rarely had a guest express an aromatic aversion.

Some people, especially winemakers, can get quite granular with their comments – chalky vs dusty tannins, for example – but I recommend keeping things simple. Describe a wine's textural elements and main tastes (sour, sweet) in terms of low, medium and high. If that feels woefully unromantic, sub in as straightforward an adjective as possible, ie 'bright acidity' instead of 'high acidity' or 'powerful' for 'rich mouthfeel and highly tannic'.

If you still feel as though you aren't getting your point across, use examples. 'This New Zealand Sauvignon Blanc is considerably zippier than that Sancerre we had the other day,' and 'I'm in the mood for something soft and plush, like a Grenache' are great examples of effective wine communication.

DESCRIBING AROMAS: ACHIEVING CLARITY THROUGH VAGUENESS

Picking individual scents out of a glass of wine can be exciting, especially if the person with whom you are enjoying the bottle has similar levels of skill and enthusiasm. But should you need to describe a wine to someone you don't know, being less specific can often bring better results.

Say you go into a restaurant and try to order a wine that smells like apple blossom. The sommelier's success in making a good recommendation hinges not only upon having smelled apple blossom before, but on being able to discern it from other similar-smelling flowers. Maybe you grew up in New England and know this scent by heart. They might be from Chicago and have only ever seen a picture of an apple tree. This is where being uber-specific in your descriptions can actually lead to miscommunications. Had you simply expressed your love of floral wines, the sommelier could likely present you with several suitable selections.

Let's change players and assume you are speaking not to a wine professional but a new friend. If you start talking about apple blossom and your companion is either unable to pick it out or, due to cultural differences, doesn't know what apple blossom smells like, they are going to disengage. If, however,

TRAINING YOUR NOSE

I give this advice all the time. If you want to become a better wine taster, become a better smeller. As previously discussed, our noses do the heavy lifting when it comes to detecting wine flavour.

Don't just smell your wine. Smell your world. I'm serious. We smell things all day that we don't necessarily consciously register. Start paying attention. How does it smell when you open that new ream of copy paper? What does your daily vitamin smell like? Your child's chalkboard? Sniff your way through the bulk grains in your local grocery store (discreetly). Try to guess what your partner is cooking using just your sense of smell. Taste a complex dish and attempt to guess the ingredients. Walk down a crowded city street on a hot summer day and try to pick out individual scents. Discern the difference between a grapefruit's flesh and its rind.

I remember the first time someone described a wine's aroma to me as 'tomato leaf', I rolled my eyes so hard they twisted in their sockets. But I also remember the first time I actually smelled the leaf of a tomato plant, and noticed how it was truly distinct from the fruit. And then considered the difference between a freshly picked, sun-warmed tomato and one pulled straight from the fridge.

The point is not necessarily to train yourself to pick out these smells from a glass of wine, but to increase your overall sensitivity. That this exercise also forces you to slow down and live in the moment is an added bonus.

Don't just smell your wine. Smell your world... Start paying attention.

you describe the wine more generally, as 'floral', you are inviting them to draw upon their own smell experience and connect with the wine. Your own appreciation might even be enriched by their perspective.

Because I spent most of my career on the consumer-facing side of the industry, I am very focused on making wine-speak as easy to understand as possible, especially in the context of a transaction. This is why I almost always prefer to use the aromatic category over the specific aroma. In my experience, it is a far more effective and less alienating way to discuss wine. Having said that, the most efficient communication is not always the most inspiring. Wine needs its poetry, too (more on that below).

AROMA CATEGORIES

The following are some common categories of wine aromas along with brief descriptions.

FRUITY

Unless a wine is old, fruit smells are present if not dominant, which makes this an essential category. But the term 'fruity' might be insufficient on its own. However unfairly, describing a wine as 'fruity' connotes that it is young and unsophisticated. Further clarification is recommended.

There are several ways to categorize fruit, but I find the most helpful to be:

- **Citrus** – lime, lemon, grapefruit, blood orange.
- **Orchard** – apple, peach, pear, quince.
- **Tropical** – banana, pineapple, guava, mango.
- **Berry** – currant, raspberry, strawberry, blueberry, goji berry.

These are broad, imperfect categories, but they can be helpful when describing wine. For example, if someone were to ask me for a citrusy white, I wouldn't necessarily need to know if they meant lime or grapefruit to put together a great list of suggestions.

Because berries are the dominant descriptors for red wine, here again some subdivision is in order. My personal preference is to refer to berry colour, such as red, blue or black. Again, this is a flawed but useful strategy. If someone asks for a red-fruited wine, I'm going to bet they are looking for a brighter, lighter style of wine like Pinot Noir. If someone asks for a black-fruited wine, I'm thinking along the lines of Cabernet Sauvignon, Petite Sirah or Aglianico.

Another point of consideration is the state of the fruit, by which I mean underripe, fresh, dried or cooked. This level of distinction may seem like a bridge too far, but you have already crossed it if you've ever described a wine as 'jammy'.

The key to becoming a great wine taster is to exercise your nose, but don't just focus on fruits and vegetables! Spices, flowers, rocks – even people and places – can pop up in a wine's bouquet.

FLORAL

Wines can evoke a whole range of flowers and while greater specificity can be useful ('dried flowers' or 'white flowers'), I believe that in most cases 'floral' alone will suffice.

SPICY

I'll start by saying that, for wine purposes, the word 'spicy' never refers to heat.

Spice is a monumental category of foodstuffs that includes such disparate members as peppercorn, vanilla, clove, anise, cumin, cardamom, bay leaf and ginger. Because of the vastness of the genre, further specificity is recommended. Here, perhaps more than anywhere else, a taster's country of origin or culture plays a role in which spice notes they might detect in a given wine.

Despite my position that the word 'spicy' is too general to be meaningful, it is found in a substantial number of tasting notes. In my experience, 'spicy' written on its own tends to refer to either peppercorns or the group of spices commonly used in western baking traditions: cinnamon, cloves and nutmeg.

I do not recommend using 'spicy' as a generic term.

EARTHY

Earthy aromas are often, but not always, found in older wines. Scents include potting soil, forest floor, adobe and mushroom. 'Earthy' on its own is sufficient shorthand in most cases.

OAKY

Oak imparts a very specific range of aromas, including vanilla, coconut, hay, smoke and fresh-sawn timber.

HERBAL/VEGETAL

There are a considerable number of herbs that can be found in wine, ranging from rosemary to mint to oregano to lavender. Herbal notes are found in white, rosé and red alike. The famous '*garrigue*' of Provençal wines is thought to be an imprint of the wild herbs that surround the vineyards, specifically lavender, rosemary and thyme.

'Herbal' is considered either a neutral or a positive attribute, but 'vegetal' tends to carry a negative connotation. In wine, the word 'vegetal' is most often used to describe Sauvignon Blanc, Cabernet Sauvignon, or a noticeably underripe wine. 'Vegetal' typically registers as 'green' and consumers rarely want green aromas in their wines, especially red wines. This is the reason that, though green pepper is an inherent characteristic of Cabernet Sauvignon, most producers de-emphasize it through their farming and winemaking decisions.

MINERAL

Mineral is a contentious term in wine, with naysayers arguing that you cannot smell minerals. Nonetheless, it has become a relatively accepted descriptor for aromas including chalk, oyster shell and wet stone.

OTHER

Other commonly accepted mini categories of wine aromas include smoky (campfire, incense, charcoal), animal (leather, sweat, blood) and nutty.

THE UNEXPECTED BENEFITS OF DEVELOPING YOUR WINE VOCABULARY

I already said that wine loves its contradictions. Well, apparently so do I. Because though I just spent the last several paragraphs decrying overly specific wine descriptors, I am now going to advocate on their behalf.

I can still remember the first time I found chamomile in a glass of Sauternes. I was groping for the word and when I finally seized it, an electric shock ran through me. Now chamomile is the first thing I notice whenever I'm lucky enough to sip this particular dessert wine.

WESTERN BIAS

Wine may not have originated in Europe, but it was the Europeans who spread it around the world during the colonial era. They brought with them not only vines and winemaking skills, but the rituals surrounding its consumption and accepted descriptive language.

Today, wine is made on all continents except Antarctica, in a staggering array of styles, by people of all cultural backgrounds. And yet, the industry continues to insist that there is a 'right' way to enjoy and describe wine. And that 'right' way is invariably Western.

Common wine descriptors favour European foodstuffs. Pairing recommendations feature European dishes (unless they are recommending Szechuan with Riesling). And our traditions of service are grounded in historic European practices. Even this book is written with a heavy Western bias, because I was born and raised inside those traditions.

But a new generation of drinkers is shaking off that long and entrenched association, preserving the elements they enjoy and creating their own traditions and descriptions. This is only good news for wine, which needs to stretch its legs.

So please. Use this book as a reference, not a rulebook. Wine can be beautiful, emotional, creative, personal. So should be your relationship with it.

What fascinates me is that the scent was there long before I could articulate it. I had been smelling it for years before I finally pinned a name on it. It felt like scanning for a radio station. I heard the distorted impression of something familiar and adjusted my frequency until the signal became clear. The song was always playing, my sensors just weren't properly in tune.

Did putting a name to the scent make the wine taste better? In a sense, it did.

My ability to isolate and describe distinct aromas increased my excitement about, engagement with, and connection to that wine. And though I try to taste as objectively as possible, I confess that it is difficult to fully subtract emotions from the equation. Feeling like I understood the wine a bit better increased my fondness for it, which became bound up in my sensory assessment of it.

The best analogy I can think of is with film. Say I am watching a movie in a language I don't speak. It may be the most beautifully shot and well-acted film in the world, but if I can't understand what is happening, I probably won't like it very much. Turn on the subtitles, however, and I'm in love.

Training your palate to better articulate wine is like turning on subtitles. It can unlock a deeper level of aesthetic appreciation.

It's worth stating that, just because I identified chamomile, doesn't mean that something is wrong with you if you don't. The point isn't to find the 'right' aroma, just to train yourself to isolate specific aromas. I smelled chamomile because I grew up drinking it; someone from a different culture, with a different culinary tradition, might detect something else. Something to which I might be oblivious. Something equally legitimate. Wine does not belong to just one people.

LETTING THE POETS IN

Effective wine communication is all about context.

First, I challenged you to find personal metaphors to help describe wine to yourself. Then I suggested that speaking in more generalized terms was the best system for communicating about wine with strangers. And then I stated that articulating wine in as detailed and precise a manner as possible was the ideal way to hone your palate and commune with wine.

Now I am going to make the case for poetry.

Is a wine simply the sum of its flavours and structural elements? Or is it something more? And if so, how best to convey that? This is where poetry comes into play. And by 'poetry' I don't necessarily mean iambic pentameter or haiku. I'm talking about the creative and emotional application of language.

Jorge Luis Borges once said of wine: 'Within your living crystal these eyes of ours have seen / a crimson metaphor.' Michael Broadbent described the massive and unconventional 1945 Château Mouton Rothschild as 'a Churchill of a wine'. A particularly lovely Napa Valley Cabernet Sauvignon inspired Regine Rousseau to pen 'the wine's centre is a deep dusty red like the streaks of lights needling through the Pétion-Ville clouds at sundown … the wine slips over the tongue like a well-enjoyed mango seed, smooth with some grit'. And Miguel de Leon once longed for a wine to make him feel like the little spoon.

Wine can evoke so much more than just a list of ingredients. It's ok to get creative with your descriptions. Ever have a wine that tasted of sunset?

Poetic wine descriptions don't have to be so overt. Consider the tasting notes in your local wine store. Ever read about a brooding wine? An introspective wine? A wine with great posture or a noble demeanor? What about a transcendent wine? An electric wine. An immortal wine. A wine that whispers, a wine that shouts. A wine that sings, soars or leaps. Architectural, harmonious, symphonic, discordant… Poetry sneaks in while we're counting the blueberries.

The descriptions above may not make literal sense upon examination. But I would argue that they convey more about the total experience of a wine than your average aromatic survey.

As Dr Shepherd himself admits: 'Connecting smells and flavour with language may be difficult, but it is a uniquely human endeavour. That we require effort to do it, using all the linguistic tricks at our disposal… qualified by the entire vocabulary of emotion… should not come, therefore, as a surprise.'

3

Buying Wine

Now that you know how to talk about what you are tasting, it's time to put those skills to work! There are several ways to purchase wine, and each comes with its own quirks and conditions.

But before I dive too deeply into the world of restaurants, retailers and professional reviews, I'll begin with a cautionary tale. Because sometimes even seasoned professionals don't know the best way to talk about wine.

HOW TO TALK TO SOMMELIERS –
AND OTHER WINE ORDERING ADVENTURES

We all have a system.

Some order the second-cheapest wine on the list. The luxe flipside of this is to seek out the second most expensive wine. Others default to the oldest vintage. Some people don't like to look at the list at all and simply hand it back, unopened, with a 'bring me your most buttery Chardonnay,' or 'do you have a dry Riesling?' or simply mutter 'red'.

When I was in my mid-twenties, I encountered an even more interesting approach. I was single, and though I had a few years of wine industry experience under my belt, I hesitated to wield my knowledge in dating situations. I didn't want to scare the poor fellas off!

So, imagine my surprise when my date ordered the perfect bottle of wine: a Mâcon-Viré-Clessé from a producer I can no longer recall. This vibrant Chardonnay was fruity but not overbearing, paired marvellously with our meal, and at around $35 was friendly to our student loan-ravaged wallets. I thought I had hit the jackpot – a cute guy who kept his car clean and sported a working knowledge of wine.

Over the next several dates, however, it became clear that he knew absolutely nothing about wine and that the first glorious selection had happened by accident. I had to know – how did he stumble upon such an ideal bottle? His answer was spectacular. 'My system,' the young man confessed, 'is to order the wine with the most accent marks.'

Fast-forward several years and I'm now a sommelier at one of New York City's most serious wine destinations. I wasn't doing the ordering, I wasn't doing the pricing, I wasn't even serving the food. My job consisted solely of trying to understand and navigate guests' palates and then select and serve them wine. 'Easy!' I thought. Not so easy.

Pity the sommelier. They truly have a difficult job. In a handful of minutes, they need to decipher your wine descriptors, figure out how much you are willing to spend, and make suggestions – all while considering the food you will eat, the weather, the nature of the occasion and a host of other variables. And inevitably, each person at the table will have their own individual palates and opinions that need to be taken into account.

I wasn't one of those rockstar sommeliers that could pour a magnum of champagne one-handed across a crowded table and never spill a drop. But I was a good sommelier in that I sincerely cared about trying to match the person in front of me to their ideal wine, rarely upsold (sorry, proprietors!), and wasn't pushing a particular agenda or ideology. But my success in effectively translating a customer's words into their dream bottle of wine was, if I'm being honest, dissatisfying in its irregularity. It took me far too long to figure out a bulletproof system of interpretation. But once I did, it was a game-changer.

And like most radical changes, it was brought about through epic failure.

My job consisted solely of trying to understand and navigate guests' palates and then select and serve them wine. 'Easy!' I thought. Not so easy...

I left New York in 2010 and moved to Napa Valley, where I helped run an all-Napa wine programme. The list was, naturally, Cabernet Sauvignon dominant. I came up with what I thought was a creative opening line that got straight to the heart of the matter. 'Would you prefer a drier, more Bordeaux-like style of Cabernet Sauvignon or a richer California style?'

I was using the word 'Bordeaux' as a kind of stylistic shorthand to indicate a leaner body, lower alcohol and earthy aromatics. But of course, I never explained this to the guest. I just assumed that they would understand. Looking back, I cringe at how overly simplistic and inaccurate this framing was (Bordeaux comes in a spectrum of styles, just like Napa Cabernet). But, as a communication strategy, it mostly worked. Until it didn't.

One night I presented a customer with this question, and she replied without hesitation: 'Oh I definitely prefer a more Bordeaux-like style of Cabernet.' I walked her through some options, and we eventually selected an older vintage from Dunn Vineyards. The wine was beautiful – austere, complex and significantly tannic – everything that I had thought this woman wanted. But she hated it. She hated it so much that she ended up hating me too.

I was determined to find out where I went wrong and so marched back to the table. In trying to find a more suitable alterative, I asked her to name a wine that she had really enjoyed recently. She replied that Joseph Phelps' Insignia was her favourite. To my palate, Insignia, while wonderful, is the epitome of a dark, luscious and fruit-driven California Cabernet. But to her it was 'dry, earthy and Bordeaux-like'. It's not that either one of us was wrong, per se. We were simply speaking different languages.

This was a moment of profound clarity for me. I realized that unless two people tasted together all the time or came from very similar cultural and professional backgrounds, it would be hard

ORDERING WINE LIKE A PRO

1 Give examples. You will experience less confusion if you are direct in your references. Saying, 'the last wine I really enjoyed was X' leaves much less to the imagination than if you were to say, 'I want something bold' or 'I want something chocolatey'.

2 Be direct about price. Tell the sommelier exactly what you want to spend or provide a range. If you don't want to say the number out loud, you can simply point to a price on the menu and say, 'I'd like to be right around here'.

3 Sample by-the-glass. It is more than OK to ask to taste multiple by-the-glass offerings before committing.

4 Ask the sommelier what excites them. Most wine lists are a combination of brands the sommelier *must* carry (due to consumer demand or other obligations), and brands the sommelier *wants* to carry. Asking this question can be a great way to discover something unexpected.

5 Don't be scared. I recently had a client tell me she was afraid to talk to sommeliers because she didn't want to seem ignorant. And this woman was a doctor! I told her that was like me not wanting to talk to her because I didn't know enough about the human body. Sommeliers (and merchants, educators, etc) are there to help. They are professional wine experts hired to share their expertise; do not hesitate to put them to the test.

Remember, your sommelier is a tool. Use them!

to understand, with any sort of precision, the other's approach to describing this mysterious beverage we call wine.

After that, my tableside approach changed significantly. 'What's the last bottle of wine that really excited you?' I would ask. No more guessing games for me.

GOOD VS BAD SOMMELIERS

In certain circles, sommeliers have a bad reputation for being pretentious or even overly mercenary. The pretentious label is understandable, given the rather precious nature of the position, but then I'm a defender of the sommelier. Are there bad ones out there? You bet! But there are bad mechanics, lawyers and sculptors, too. I once had a doctor take a personal call on their cell phone mid-diagnosis.

It's truly hard to not alienate your audience when talking about wine. A technical approach (scent of cherries, medium acidity) can sound just as bizarre as more emotional appeals (a transcendent wine that speaks of its terroir) if the person to whom you are speaking does not share the depth of your passion. Which is why the best sommeliers are listeners first, storytellers second. Not everyone comes to a restaurant to learn.

HOW TO TELL IF YOU HAVE A BAD SOMMELIER?

- **Unreasonable upsell** If you tell them what you want to spend and they offer you something considerably more pricey, that's a bad sommelier.

    A small increase is understandable, especially if it can be justified based on quality; but a big jump means they either aren't listening or don't have your best interests in mind.

- **Talking schist** If your sommelier goes into unprompted technical detail, especially if they start naming obscure soils *without saying what exact qualities that brings to the glass*, that's a bad sommelier.

    An engaged and eager guest is a sommelier's dream and some customers really do want to geek out. But many people just want to order a wine quickly and return to their conversation. Oftentimes, the best thing a sommelier can say is: 'Excellent choice.'

- **Deliberate mismatching of wine to palate** Communication breakdowns are inevitable, but some sommeliers get so excited about a particular trend, style or category of wine that they lose sight of the guest.

  A friend of mine recently explained to a sommelier that she didn't care for any overt 'funkiness' in wine only to be presented with a series of truly edgy pairings. Similarly, one should never serve a soft and fruity Merlot to a natural wine fanatic. The guests' preferences should be paramount.

One big caveat to this is that not all restaurants have extensive wine lists, and some have a very specific point of view. My all-Napa wine list certainly didn't have something for everyone, so a guest in that situation must surrender at least a little bit to what's on offer. Similar advice applies to those visiting restaurants with natural wine lists, which are increasingly popular.

...the best sommeliers are listeners first, storytellers second. "

RESTAURANT FAQs

Restaurants are incredible places. The best ones are vibrant, welcoming, nourishing community centres that contribute to a neighborhood's character. I've watched people get engaged, helped an elderly pair celebrate 50 years of marriage and witnessed countless couples fall in love before my very eyes. One time, the entire cycle of life transpired in a single week – I called an ambulance when a man went into cardiac arrest, cleaned up after a woman's waters broke and walked in on a couple attempting to – presumably – conceive a child. A lot of life happens in restaurants.

Some people dine out every night; others save up all year for one single special meal. But I get asked by even the most seasoned diners about practices surrounding wine in restaurants. I understand why. The rules can seem somewhat muddy and up for interpretation, especially when policies shift from not only country to country, but business to business. Because of this, though I attempt to clarify and advise below, one should always check in with the specific restaurant before making assumptions about corkage and the like.

SHOULD I SNIFF THE CORK?

No. Many people assume that you are supposed to sniff the cork to see if the wine is sound, but that's not how the tradition arose. Historically, corks were presented to safeguard against fraud. Is the right vintage/producer/vineyard listed on the cork? Does it appear to have been tampered with? These were the considerations to watch out for, not its odour. Besides, the best way to tell if a wine is suffering from cork taint is to smell the wine itself. I've experienced terribly tainted bottles with corks that smelled as fresh as daisies. So, skip sniffing the cork and dig into the glass instead.

WHY IS WINE SO MUCH MORE EXPENSIVE IN RESTAURANTS THAN IN RETAIL?

Restaurant economics, at least in the United States, are bleak. According to the National Restaurants Association, the average pre-tax profitability in 2022 was only around five percent. This slim margin creates all sorts of instability in the industry. The side effects are many, but chief among them are an over-reliance on tips to compensate employees, and wine prices that are significantly higher than retail average. Because there is greater price literacy around food, wine bears the brunt of the markup to cover what is traditionally an astonishingly high cost of doing business.

WHAT IS A CORKAGE FEE AND WHY SHOULD I PAY IT?

'Corkage' is when a guest opts to bring their own bottle into a restaurant, and that privilege usually comes with a fee. In my time as a sommelier, the most heated arguments I witnessed usually involved a customer resenting a corkage fee. Though I understand that it may seem unreasonable to be charged money to consume your own wine, restaurants often have important reasons for doing so. It is also worthwhile noting that not all businesses allow this practice, and in some places it is even illegal. In short, call your restaurant to make sure it is permitted before carrying in your own wine.

Reasons to charge corkage include:

- **Breakage** You may be bringing in your own bottle, but you are drinking it out of the restaurant's glassware. And, depending on the place, a hand-blown crystal stem can cost up to $50 apiece. No matter how well-trained and careful the staff, breakage is an almost daily occurrence. Your corkage fee helps offset this.

- **Labour** Most likely, a sommelier or waiter is opening and pouring your wine all night. If you bring in a special, older wine that requires skilled handling of the cork and/or decanting, that takes time and expertise.

- **Displaced business** The truth of the matter is, if every customer brought in their own wine, most (fine dining) restaurants would go out of business. As elucidated above, wine markups are often calculated to cover business expenses that simply can't be tacked onto the price of the food. So, in addition to covering hard costs like breakage, a corkage fee can also serve as a deterrent. This doesn't mean that it's wrong or bad to bring in your own wine, especially if you are a regular, tip well, or order additional wine. My intention here is to simply explain a business practice that can often result in confusion and discontentment on the part of the guest.

WHY DO SOME SOMMELIERS TASTE THE WINE BEFORE THE GUEST?

Another controversial sommelier move. Not all sommeliers will smell/taste a wine before serving it to the guest, but I am emphatically in favour of the practice. Why? Because sommeliers are specifically trained to seek out flaws including but not limited to cork taint. Plus, ideally, they have familiarity with the wines on their list and should know how they are supposed to taste. Skipping this step lays all the responsibility on the guest, who may or may not be equipped to detect flaws. Aside from the educational benefits for the sommelier tasting the wine, there are two negative consequences this practice avoids.

- **One** A sommelier may have just sold someone the perfect wine, a wine that ought to inspire and uplift them and elevate their meal to previously unknown aesthetic heights. Imagine the bottle is corked, but the guest doesn't know what cork taint smells like. They might just think they don't like this wine or that the sommelier has no idea what they are talking about. That's bad for them, bad for the sommelier, bad for the restaurant and bad for the winery.

- **Two** Let's say the guest *does* know what a cork taint smells like. They send the wine back and a second unblemished bottle is produced. No harm, no foul, right? Wrong. The guest now has a negative association with this restaurant that is built into their memory of the evening. This effect became clear to me when speaking to a friend who had recently dined at a three Michelin starred restaurant. I asked them how their meal was and they immediately told me that their wine was corked. They got a new bottle and everything else was great, but that was the first comment they offered. We are wired to remember the negative, no matter how small. A preemptive sip by a sommelier, to me, is an essential act of high-touch hospitality.

DO WINES BY-THE-GLASS OFFER THE GREATEST VALUE?

Simply answered, no. Wines by-the-glass (BTG) serve a variety of functions. They can represent comfortable, familiar categories of wine to put the average consumer at ease. Or they may be a chance for the sommelier to introduce something obscure and delicious to an audience that might be shy to commit to a whole bottle. Either way, hopefully they are selected to pair with specific dishes. Having said that, opening a bottle to serve by the glass comes with a risk of spoilage, and this is typically accounted for in the price. It is not uncommon, at least in the United States, for the price of a glass of wine to be equivalent to the wholesale cost of the bottle. In this way, if someone sells a single glass of wine and the rest of the bottle goes bad because it is unused, the costs are covered. The restaurant may not have made any money on the wine, but it didn't lose any either.

WHAT'S THE DIFFERENCE BETWEEN A SOMMELIER, A MASTER SOMMELIER, AND A MASTER OF WINE?

First, let's define the word 'sommelier', since this has evolved significantly over the course of my career. When I started in the wine industry in 2001, a sommelier meant only one thing: a restaurant employee dedicated to wine service. Most restaurants don't have a sommelier, relying instead on waiters, managers or bartenders to deal with wine. By contrast, some high-end dining establishments employ a whole fleet.

Today, the term has expanded out from the confines of restaurants into the greater world of wine, and sometimes beyond wine itself; dispensaries occasionally offer 'weed sommeliers' and I recently ate at a restaurant with a 'meat sommelier'. Retailers, tasting room attendants, wine educators and influencers sometimes refer to themselves as sommeliers, often to the irritation of those still working 'on the floor', as restaurant service is often called.

Personally, I have no problem with non-restaurant workers using the title 'sommelier' to connote wine expertise. But I also don't think it does the industry any favours. Applying a hard-to-pronounce French word to fancify your position feels pretentious and exclusionary, the exact qualities that turn so many away from wine in the first place.

The sudden popularity and broad application of the term 'sommelier' likely stems from the 2012 documentary *Somm*. The film followed four men as they took their Master Sommelier exam and catapulted a rather obscure certification system into the international spotlight.

The spiking awareness of Master Sommeliers was an interesting transition to live through. I first began working as a sommelier in 2009 and none of my friends had any idea what I did for a living ('you're a somma-*what*?'). And then suddenly every guest at the restaurant believed I was a Master Sommelier, an assumption I had to wearily deny, night after night.

So, what is the difference between a sommelier and a Master Sommelier (MS)? Simply put: a Master Sommelier passed a test. Granted, it's a very hard test. But you do not need a Master Sommelier certification to work as a sommelier. And you don't even need to work as a sommelier to pass the Master Sommelier exam. In fact, many of the most talented sommeliers I know have zero interest in pursuing the Master Sommelier title, even though it can often result in a significant salary bump.

I liken it to an MBA – a useful degree that implies a certain level of scholarship, but one does not need an MBA to run a business. And just like an MBA, the MS takes considerable time and money to achieve, which favours the well-resourced.

Presenting the bottle to the guest is an elegant to way to confirm that the sommelier heard you correctly and fetched the correct bottle.

But what about a Master of Wine (MW)? How is that different from a Master Sommelier?

In the wine industry, we sometimes make things more confusing than they need to be. Certifications are no exception. As with the MS, an MW is someone that passed a really hard series of tests designed to ascertain expertise in wine. Both societies were established in England, with the Institute of Masters of Wine forming in 1953 and the Court of Master Sommeliers in 1977 (the separate American chapter was founded in 1987). Both the MW and MS titles indicate that the holder is among the most knowledgeable wine connoisseurs in the world. That said, the MS is more for restaurant professionals while the MW is industry wide.

The takeaway here is that it is reasonable to expect an MS or MW to know *a lot* about wine. But there are also world-class professionals who are not interested in pursuing those credentials.

CAN I PRE-ORDER WINE IN A RESTAURANT?

Yes! Well, sometimes. Depending on the place.

There's no sadder sight in a restaurant than the bored, forlorn face of a wine geek's partner. We used to call them 'wine widows' – rather sexist in retrospect – the abandoned date who would look around politely while their partner combed over the wine list or endlessly grilled the sommelier. The second saddest sight is the panic-stricken host who has absolutely no idea what to order, is clearly overwhelmed by the process, but needs to maintain composure in front of their guests. Both these scenarios would be solved by a quick phone call to the sommelier.

Because they are most often seen flitting around the dining room floor, many consumers don't realize that sommeliers spend considerable time in an office. But it was there, behind the desk, that I had many of my favourite wine conversations. Ringing up a sommelier to make a selection in advance is a brilliant move on a lot of levels. First, you have the undivided attention of the sommelier, who would otherwise be juggling the wishes of multiple guests at the same time. Second, you have a private audience in which to ask any questions you may like, thereby avoiding potential public embarrassment. Third, the sommelier can open your wine well in advance, if advisable.

I loved taking wine orders by phone. If a guest called to arrange for a young Barolo that I knew needed air, I could have that bottle open and decanted hours in advance. Then, the second they arrived, I could fill everyone's glasses with the champagne we'd pre-selected before menus were even cracked, and the Barolo would be perfectly ready for the main course. The host looked like royalty and had more time to converse with their dining companions, and I was free to tend to others. It was a win-win, every time.

> **Ringing up a sommelier to make a selection in advance is a brilliant move on a lot of levels.**

WHAT IF THERE IS NO SOMMELIER?

If you go to a restaurant and it either doesn't have a sommelier or they're off-duty, ask a manager, bartender or server for assistance. But if you are truly on your own, try taking *one step into the unknown*.

Here is what I mean. Say you love South African Chenin Blanc. You don't see one on the list, but they do have a Chenin Blanc from the Loire Valley. Try it! You at least have a reference point to compare it against. Or maybe you see a different wine from your favourite Chenin Blanc producer. Try it! Or perhaps you don't see any of the above, but the restaurant does offer a different South African selection. Try it! Ordering a wine that is at least tangentially related to something you love is a better strategy than closing your eyes and pointing to a random selection.

SHOULD I TIP ON THE WINE?

This is a very personal subject, and readers will have to make up their own minds. I discuss my practices below but, speaking as a former sommelier, the hope is that you will include the price of the wine in your bill when calculating the tip. A common follow-up question is, what if it's a very expensive bottle? Again, personal judgement should guide you here, but to me, that's like asking if people who make more money should receive a lower tax rate. Oh wait…

WHAT DO 'YOU' DO?

It's all well and good to lecture others on their habits, but it's far more important to walk the actual walk. So rather than deliver a sermon on what I think best practices should be, I'll simply describe the way I approach things in my household, and why.

● **Tips** Before travelling, I research the average tip rate of my destination (20 percent in the United States) and then treat that as part of the bill. If the experience was exceptional and I want to recognize that with a larger tip, I will do so. But I never use the tip to punish, even in instances of bad service. Why? In my time as a sommelier in New York City and Napa Valley, I probably made more than almost anyone else in the restaurant. And I still had a heck of a time covering my bills. Restaurant positions may offer plenty of wonderful experiences and benefits, but a truckload of money is rarely one of them. Besides, making front-of-house staff reliant on tips to earn their living sets up a problematic dynamic between guest and staff and often makes the employee feel disempowered to speak up for themselves or call-out bad behaviour. As I said before, restaurant economics are broken. Until they are fixed, tip your server the full amount.

- **Corkage** My husband is also in the wine industry. Hopefully, you don't come knocking on our door with a medical emergency – we will not be able to assist you. But if you are thirsty, we have you covered. Our house is crammed full of wine, and yet we rarely bring wine into restaurants. We feel that a wine programme is often (not always!) as fundamental a part of a restaurant's expression as the cuisine. In the rare instance that we do bring in a wine, we always make sure to buy a bottle. So, if we are bringing in a red, we'll buy a white or champagne, and vice versa. We always tip on the wine, and if bringing in a corkage bottle, we tip extra heavy to compensate for the lost sale.

RETAIL: THE FRONTLINES OF CONSUMER ENGAGEMENT

When it comes to learning about wine, nothing beats a local shop.

You might see your favourite sommelier a couple of times a year but, depending on your drinking habits, you could visit a retailer as often as once a week. And connecting with a specific employee at your neighbourhood wine store is the fastest track to personalized wine instruction. Not to mention a bounty of tasty bottles.

Wine shops come in all shapes and sizes. At the bulbous end of the spectrum, chain outlets and supermarkets might stock fewer interesting options, but the pricing tends to be competitive. On the boutique side of things, there is often more of an editorial perspective.

Within 30 miles of my house, for example, there are several wine stores. One is dedicated to local Napa Valley wines, which tend to carry a higher price point; one focuses on natural wines; one offers eclectic international wines; one is a big box retailer that only carries ubiquitous mass-produced brands; and one is a supermarket where I know I can get a handful of household favourites at the lowest prices around. There are also a couple of locally based virtual merchants who offer robust online selections but no physical shelves to browse. Granted, I live in wine country, so the landscape is especially boozy, but many neighbourhoods offer at least a couple of options.

With so many possibilities, how do you choose? I would argue that your personal relationship with a merchant is as important as the selections they carry.

Here is why. A great wine merchant will seek to understand your palate. They will track your orders and walk with you on your journey from wine-curious to wine-confident. In turn, it is your responsibility to provide them with honest and constructive feedback and – ideally – reward their attention with your loyalty.

Your local wine shop might even offer services beyond single bottle recommendations. It certainly doesn't hurt to ask. I know of several stores that put together lesson plans in the form of mixed cases, complete with written material on the wines. At the very least, it is common for retailers to host regular public tastings and may even feature visiting winemakers. This last bit is an invaluable way to appreciate wine on a deeper level, especially if you've never travelled to a wine-producing region. At my first retail gig, I used to host tastings that matched wine with music. If you didn't know that AC/DC is the perfect pairing for Hunter Valley Semillon, now you do.

In short, go find a store – better yet, a person at a store – that you trust, even if it means travelling slightly out of your way. Wine books are great, but nothing beats a personal recommendation from a knowledgeable salesperson who has taken the time to get to know your preferences.

Browsing the shelves of a well-curated boutique wine shop can be a great way to familiarize yourself with a range of wines and labels.

At my first retail gig, I used to host tastings that matched wine with music.

A NOTE ON IMPORTERS AND DISTRIBUTORS

Here's how the wine industry typically works: a producer sells to an importer who sells to a distributor who sells to a restaurant or retailer who sells to you. Sometimes these steps are merged. For example, certain importers do their own distribution, or a retailer might import specific brands directly. But, generally speaking, a wine passes through many hands before it reaches your lips, and at each stage a cut is taken. This is a part of the reason why wines are often more expensive outside their native countries.

Top restaurants and retailers purchase from a broad range of distributors in order to provide their customers with the best selections. Casting such a wide net translates to considerable extra work for the buyer – more relationships to maintain, more tastings, more paperwork, more time. It is far easier to rely on a single portfolio of wines – and some places do – but the results are inevitably dull.

Distribution is typically invisible to consumers, but importers can become as famous as the wines they sell. And their connections to wineries are better established in large part because the importer is often listed on the wine label, typically on the back.

I started my career in retail and got to know wine by drinking my way through the shop. Eventually, I noticed that many of my favourite wines had the same back label. It didn't take me long to figure out that they were all brought in by the same importer, and that importers have preferences, just like people. Some importers, especially the larger ones, might seek to cover all bases and bring in a vast range of wines. Others zero in on a particular region, style or philosophy.

My first favourite importers focused almost exclusively on small production, family-run French and Italian wineries that farmed in a holistic way. The wines often skewed towards elegant and were rarely overly-alcoholic or excessively oaky, which was right up my alley. As a new wine drinker, this was a profound realization. I discovered a lot of exciting wines by looking up what other producers those importers carried.

To this day, if I'm in a wine shop and can't find somebody to help me, I instinctively start turning over bottles and reading the back label. If I see that a wine is brought in by an importer I trust, I'll buy it.

HOW ARE WINES PRICED?

I can still remember the time an angry man flagged me down, pointed to the wine list, and asked: 'Are you seriously telling me this $1,000 bottle of wine is 10 times better than this $100 bottle?' Followed by an enraged. 'Is it going to get me 10 times as drunk?'

He was furious, deeply offended that anyone would charge so much for a single bottle of wine. I supplied a poorly thought-out analogy comparing coach versus business flights (they both get you there at the same time!), but he wasn't actually interested in having a conversation. Still, it's a subject I've thought a lot about since.

Why *do* some wines cost more than others? It's a simple question that generates a complex answer. But I'll do my best to break down the different elements here.

FARMING

This is a pivotal issue. Simply put, it is more expensive to farm by hand than it is to mechanize, and it is significantly more costly to farm naturally than it is to spray a bunch of pesticides, herbicides and fungicides onto the vines. One winery I know saw their farming costs go up eight times when they switched from using Round-Up to hand-hoeing weeds. Eight times!

VINEYARD LABOUR

Many wineries rely on transient or migrant labour in the vineyards because there are only a handful of times a year when a large workforce is required, such as harvest. But some wineries opt instead to take on the added expense of retaining their crew year-round, providing benefits and job security. Beyond the vineyard, a winery might spend more on labour to attract top winemakers, consultants, cellar workers, salespeople and even a hospitality team if they are open to the public.

It can be easy to forget that wine is an agricultural product. The longer I am in the industry, the more important quality farming has become to me.

EQUIPMENT

Equipment expenses can range from such everyday items as fermentation tanks and tractors up to specialized gear like optical grape sorters and laboratory instruments. How tech-forward a winery is may also affect the final bottle price.

MATERIALS

These are items that need to be regularly re-purchased, such as barrels, glass bottles, corks – even grapes, if a winery doesn't own their vineyards. And these expenses can really range. New oak barrels can cost over $1,000 each, older or 'neutral' barrels are far less, and oak products such as chips, staves and powder are the cheapest by far (and taste accordingly). Natural corks can cost as little as $0.06 or as much as $2.50 each. And grapes can range from a couple of hundred to tens of thousands of dollars per ton, depending on the variety and region (note: a ton generates roughly 50 cases, or 600 bottles, of wine).

OUTLET

As previously discussed, a wine's price will vary based on where you buy it. Restaurants generally charge more than retailers, and wines tend to increase in price once they leave their country of origin.

INTANGIBLE FACTORS

The above represent hard costs. But there are invisible elements that also contribute to the price of a wine such as reputation, rarity, critical reception, pedigree, emotional impact and aesthetic value. Time is also a consideration, with older vintages often selling for more than current releases, assuming the wine is known to age well.

For some wines, especially those that are mass-produced, prices can be very closely tied to production costs. But for many other wines, at both the high and the low end of the spectrum, pricing typically involves at least a few intangible factors.

So, considering it is possible to buy a bottle of wine for as little as a few dollars, why would anyone spend more? Especially when, according to my angry customer, it won't get you any more drunk?

The answer is not just because the wine is better, though quality is certainly a factor, but because it makes you *feel* something.

It's true. One person might spend more on a bottle of wine because it makes them feel smart; because they believe the wine is worth far more than its price tag implies. Another person might spend more on a bottle of wine because of its sentimental value, be it a connection to the winery, the vintage, a trip, or a memorable meal. Yet another person might spend more on a bottle of wine because it communicates something about their social or economic status, while someone else might spend more if they know the winery is farming or conducting business according to certain principles.

I spend money on wine because I love it, and because a great bottle can move me as much as any other work of art. Sometimes that bottle costs a little, sometimes considerably more. Taste alone has historically been my guide, but over time I've given extra weight to wines whose price tags also cover impeccable farming and well-compensated employees.

One wine costs more than another for a variety of reasons, but greatness can be found at many price points. You should neither feel pressured to spend more than you should nor shamed into spending less than you are inclined to. Like all other decisions in wine, what you spend on a bottle needs to make sense for your palate, your priorities, your wallet and your life.

Barrels, bungs, tanks, racks, architecture, pedigree, reputation, the value of the land and and the age of the business can all contribute to the final cost of a wine.

CHOOSE-YOUR-OWN ADVENTURE!
LEARNING ABOUT WINE ONE BOTTLE AT A TIME

Did you ever read those choose-your-own adventure books as a kid? The kind where at the conclusion of each chapter your character had to make a choice that informed the ending? I loved those books and would read them over and over, trying all the permutations until I got to the best possible outcome.

I recommend a similar strategy with wine.

If by chance you stumble across a bottle you really like, make a note, snap a picture, whatever you need to do to preserve the details. Be sure to look at the back label too. The information you glean will help guide your decision-making process so that the next time you step into a shop or open a wine list, you aren't starting from scratch.

I like to think of each bottle of wine as a collection of data points, some of which are more meaningful than others. Most wines clearly advertise their producer, region of origin, grape variety or blend, vintage, price and so on. They may also disclose the vineyard source, importer, winemaker, and the style or philosophy behind the wine (natural, organic, biodynamic, low alcohol, etc).

Treat this tasty wine like the first chapter in a choose-your-own adventure novel. Each data point you follow will lead you down a different path. If you go one direction and don't like the outcome, backtrack and start again.

An example: Imagine the wine that stole your heart is a Catena 'High Mountain Vineyards' Malbec from Mendoza, Argentina. From there you might decide to explore the grape variety Malbec, which could send you to Bordeaux, or towards its origin, the more obscure Cahors region of France. Or perhaps you fix your attention on Argentina and see what else it has to offer. Though it was a hearty red that turned your head, you may find yourself entranced by the country's many distinctively floral Torrontés whites. Alternatively, you could decide to focus on the producer and discover that, while the Malbec was great, your favourite is actually their Cabernet Franc, which might, in turn, lead you to this grape's spiritual home, the Loire Valley in France. If you get super geeky, you could even find yourself investigating other high-elevation wines. Be sure to also make note of wines you dislike, as there's information to be mined there as well.

Now let's select a white.

Say you decide to splurge on an Albert Boxler Brand vineyard Grand Cru Riesling from Alsace, France. As with the Malbec, you might set off to explore Rieslings from around the world. But this wine has the added complexity of coming from an officially designated Grand Cru vineyard. So perhaps you start chasing other Grand Cru wines from Alsace or even zero in on those specifically from the Brand vineyard. Several other excellent producers, such as Zind-Humbrecht and Josmeyer, produce a Brand, and comparing those wines to each other would make for a fascinating tasting. Assuming you are drinking this bottle in America, you might turn it over and note that it is imported by Kermit Lynch. This could inspire you to check out other wines from his catalogue, which may lead you to Corsica or Provence. Or a deep dive into Boxler may reveal that it is farmed biodynamically, which sends you searching all over the globe for other wines farmed according to this philosophy. Every step you take outwards from that first bottle unlocks its own world of options. But in a manageable, methodical way.

Over the course of this exercise, you will learn a lot about your preferences. You will also become more wine-confident and wine-fluent. Remember: it's impossible to learn everything about wine. The key is to explore, have fun and stay curious. Your relationship with wine will hopefully be a long one, but all stories need to start somewhere. This one begins with a single bottle.

INSIDE TRACK
QUALITY VS PREFERENCE

In my mind, the biggest difference between wine consumers and wine professionals boils down to this idea of quality vs preference. If you are buying wine for yourself, preference is everything. One of my best friend's favourite wines is a $10 sparkling pineapple wine from Hawaii. Whether I agree that it's delicious is beside the point (I do, it's quite yummy); her palate is all that matters.

But when you are buying wine for other people, or professionally reviewing a range of wines, you need to at least try to divorce your personal preference from the equation. You need to start considering a wine's inherent quality rather than its level of personal appeal. Training for this is great for your palate. Focusing on preference narrows the world of wine considerably; seeking to objectively measure quality widens the frame. Who knows? You may decide you'd been overly dismissive of a particular wine style and expand your drinking habits accordingly.

You need to start considering a wine's inherent quality rather than its level of personal appeal. Training for this is great for your palate.

STRATEGIES FOR KEEPING WINE NOTES

There are so many wines out there; even if you only try three a week, that quickly becomes too much for one mind to contain. So how do you keep track of your thoughts and observations? There are several different approaches.

OLD SCHOOL

Notebooks! In my household, nothing beats analogue, and we have several storage boxes in the garage stuffed full of old wine notebooks. But though I love to sentimentally flip through them, it's impossible to look anything up. So, unless you also happen to employ the Dewey Decimal system, something a bit higher tech might be in order.

Word or Excel A Word document or Excel spreadsheet is an excellent way to track wine notes, especially if you store it on Dropbox or some other cloud-based system (I also have a box in the garage full of old hard drives). Excel is especially useful if you graduate to the point of employing a professional inventory management system, as spreadsheets can often be easily uploaded.

NEW SCHOOL

Photos Sommelier and wine writer Miguel de Leon once bowled over a room of wine journalists when he shared that, assuming you have a smart phone, you can simply swipe up on your photo of a wine label and type in searchable notes. This feature is especially handy if you find yourself sampling dozens of wines in one go.

Website or app As we'll discuss on page 100, there are several sites and apps that allow you to record and share your own wine reviews. This is a very efficient way to store and organize your notes. Some of the apps will even fill in data like the producer and vintage if you upload a photo of the label.

CRITICS, SCORES, WINE MEDIA AND YOU

It used to be that a handful of powerful critics dominated wine media. These days, the landscape is far more fragmented. This is good news for consumers, who can shop for a critic the same way they shop for a bottle of wine.

You could learn about wine exclusively on social media today if you wanted to. The rise of influencers, apps and crowd-sourced wine reviews (explained below) has thrown the whole notion of professional wine criticism into question. Why should you care what one single person has to say about the 2010 Il Poggione Brunello di Montalcino when you can read reviews by nearly 700 different people on CellarTracker?

This is a legitimate question. I personally find crowd-sourced wine reviews very useful, especially for real-time insight into how an older bottle is drinking today. But I still firmly believe in the essential role of the critic. There is a big difference between a wine collector who purchases and opens a couple of hundred bottles a year and a professional who dedicates their life to travelling the world, walking vineyards, debating with vintners and sampling thousands of wines.

Because the wine world is so much larger than it was even a generation ago, modern critics tend to specialize in a handful of regions. And as most publications want broad coverage, they often hire a suite of reviewers to tackle as much of the world as possible. This means that, if you are interested in a particular area, the chances are good that it is covered by more than one critic. This is beneficial in that it provides an opportunity to compare different reviews of a wine you enjoy and find the writer whose tastes most closely mirror your own. For though critics work hard to separate preference from quality in their assessments, variation between palates is inevitable.

By taking honest stock of a selection of wines and comparing my notes with the views of the critics, I have figured out whose palates align with mine. And that makes their scores extremely useful to me. There are specific critics I follow for burgundy, for Australia, for blue-chip Italy, and so on. If, for example, my preferred Bordeaux critic gives a Pauillac a high rating, I pay attention. Same for when they recommend a new producer.

Which brings us to scores. Scores are a particularly contentious subject within the wine community. Detractors lament the reduction of a wine to a single number. They argue that it is a gross oversimplification that fails to convey the complexity contained in a glass of wine. Critics often retort that the context and poetry of a wine is delivered within the tasting note. To which the naysayers reply that nobody reads the note, they just look at the numbers.

Another criticism levied at scores is that the 100-point scale is really a 15-point scale, since it is unusual to see a rating of less than 85. I hear less grumbling about the British 20-point scale but still, single-digit ratings are rare. People have also complained that scores are too powerful, and that they favour established regions, varieties, producers and styles.

Being a wine professional, I rarely consider a wine's rating. I don't need to! I have a lifetime of tastings, travel and research to support my decision-making. But in almost all other areas of my life, I love professional criticism. Because in most other fields I am not an expert.

For example, I recently ordered a kazoo for my daughter. I spent 45 minutes reading reviews before pressing the pay button. And I'm glad I did – it's a mighty fine kazoo. For larger purchases, such as a car, I may spend weeks or months in search-mode. When travelling to a new city, I over-analyze the restaurant scene, cross-referencing official critiques against consumer testimonials.

On multiple occasions, I have spent more time reading about a particular restaurant than actually inside it.

In all the instances above, I relied on professional ratings to avoid wasting money and time. I understand why some people decry wine scores, but honestly feel they do more good than harm. Wine can be scary when you are just beginning… there's so much of it out there! Tasting notes and their scores help simplify a complex subject and render it far more manageable.

So please: if you are new to wine, consider scores. They are a very good way to discover new wines. Do they offer a perfect system? No. Are there other ways to learn about wine? Absolutely. But until you find your footing, relying on the collective expertise of professional wine critics is a great way to start. Especially if you find one with whom you resonate.

TASTING NOTES

At their best, tasting notes should combine one part poetry with two parts useful takeaways. They should endeavour to describe the look, smell, taste and texture of a given wine as accurately as possible and provide a sense of the wine's overall quality. Some tasting notes address relative value while others are 'price blind'; I find the former to be far more beneficial to the consumer.

Reviews read in isolation – on a retail shelf or winery website – can be helpful, but the best publications complement them with in-depth vintage assessments and regional reporting. If you are just looking for a quick Tuesday night wine, you might not require this degree of context. But if you are actively working to expand your wine knowledge, such accounts can be great resources.
It's worth highlighting that most scores are relative to their respective categories. By which I mean, 92 points is not the same

A WINE IS NOT A PAINTING
(A VAGUELY PRETENTIOUS AND SELF-INDULGENT TANGENT)

The relative value of aesthetic objects is always going to be at least partially subjective; but that doesn't render expertise futile. Similarly, critical consensus that one artist is better than another – or of a similar level of talent – is important; but that doesn't make personal preference meaningless.

I liken it to the art world. Monet and Picasso are both considered geniuses, but they present very different styles of art. Chances are that any given person has a strong preference for one over the other. Or they may dislike both and seek something else entirely! In this way, wine is a lot like a painting.

But here is where wine and art diverge.

A great work might hang in a museum or gallery. You can visit it as often as you like – in sun, in rain, at night, during the day, after a breakup, after a promotion. The painting remains the same, the only variable in your enjoyment is you.

Wine, however, is a moving target. A great wine might age slowly, but it never stands still. You behave similarly. Both you and the wine go through endless phases, endless moods. You may buy a bottle to age today but when you finally open it, neither you nor the wine are the same as before. This is a part of wine's sentimental gravity. It compels us to remember who we were the last time we tasted it, and to contemplate the intervening transformation.

I would also argue that our relationship with wine is more intimate than our relationship to art. You might invite a painting to live in your house, but we invite wine into our bodies. We share it with people we love; we give it permission to temporarily alter our brain chemistry. Our connection to a given work of art may last longer, but it doesn't run nearly as deep.

grade for a Chilean Carignan as it is for a burgundy. Outside of a 'classic' region, a score of 92 points indicates that a wine is high quality and exciting. Meanwhile, if a First Growth Bordeaux were rated 92 points, that would be considered a rather poor showing.

CROWD-SOURCING AND INFLUENCERS

In the beginning, God created the internet. And on the second day, men began gathering in chat rooms to exchange notes on wine.

Since the earliest days of the internet, there have been lively online wine debates. And this banter can be extremely informative. While I tend to look to critics and wine writers, there are some very knowledgeable collectors and connoisseurs out there with valuable perspectives to share. I also find the amateur's take interesting, especially in aggregate. This is where crowd-sourcing sites and apps come into play.

Crowd-sourcing apps and websites have become valuable tools for consumers. Unlike many wine publications, the subscription fees are either low or non-existent, and they allow the user to actively participate in a global wine discussion. With some services, you can simply scan the label of a wine and instantly access the opinions of hundreds of other imbibers. You can also upload, rate and comment upon your own wines as you go. This is not only a fun and useful exercise, but also a great way to keep track of bottles you enjoy.

Influencers are another relatively recent phenomenon. Definitions vary, but influencers tend to communicate via social media and do not function as professional critics. They can still be knowledgeable, however, and some are very powerful. In the past several years, a handful of prominent sommeliers have exerted measurable impact on the wine market through their social media campaigns and they can be thought of as a type of influencer. But typical influencers are generally less geeky and more lifestyle oriented. Followers should be mindful that social media promotions might be paid for, which legally ought to be indicated by the inclusion of '#Ad'.

STORYTELLING

Wine is an intricately layered subject. At its surface – the moment of consumer interface – lies its tastes and smells. For many, this is the depth of their consideration, and these are hardly shallow waters.

As a drinker's excitement grows, they may decide to learn about the places that produce all those beautiful wines. The histories, soils and traditions. The methods of farming. The various climates.

Then, of course, there is the manner in which a wine is made. As a former sommelier, this was regularly a point of emphasis. How much new oak and for how long, cultured vs ambient yeast, the type of fermentation tank, varietal composition, how the berries are sorted, and so on.

All of the above are profoundly interesting lines of inquiry. But the more time I spend in the wine industry, the more I realize that you can't fully separate the wine from the craft of the maker, the intention of the proprietor, or the skill of the farmer. So many hands touch a wine along its journey from dream to glass, and there are endless stories to tell.

As much as I love thinking about and drinking wine, it's the people that keep me coming back. The best wine writing emphasizes this, and the best wines – at least to me – are those that carry with them some sort of human connection. I want my sommelier to tell me a little snippet about the person who made the wine. I want to seek out wines from sentimental vintages. And I want to see the faces of the farmers on the website.

I think of wine as a branch of the humanities, and its humanity is divine.

Wine may be a natural product, but it requires human intervention to exist.

4

Handling Wine

Over the course of my career, I have fielded more questions about the practical aspects of wine appreciation than any other topic. From decanting, to selecting glassware, to pairing wine with food, the physical act of serving wine seems to be as overwhelming as deciphering a German wine label. But it doesn't need to be!

In the forthcoming pages, I will attempt to explain these concepts in a straightforward way. And to simplify them for easy application in the home.

Before we start, it's important to note that many of these traditions are just that – traditions. That is, they are the historic practices of specific cultures and peoples. While in the United States we tend to employ the European tradition of pouring women's wine first, other cultures prioritize elders. And while most of us wouldn't dream of drinking wine from a water glass, that's what you're most likely to be served it in in the many trattorias of Italy.

Furthermore, some of the more timeless-seeming aspects of wine appreciation are actually quite modern. For example, crystal clear varietally-specific wine glasses only date back to the late 1950s. Prior to that, wine was often drunk from heavily ornate and sometimes coloured glasses or goblets. Did those consumers enjoy their wines any less?

Because I was raised in the Western wine tradition, that is my focus. But it's important to recognize that there are no universal truths in wine. Which means you should feel free to adopt the practices that resonate with you and invent your own traditions as you go. The wine world needs less anxiety and more playfulness! So, take the following with a grain of salt.

A MINIMALIST'S GUIDE TO WINE GEAR

There is a massive (and growing!) wine accessory industry out there and it is increasingly difficult to navigate the congestion. Yes, some of these items will improve your wine life dramatically. But just as many, if not more, are a waste of money.

My home doesn't have a lot of space, and I'm a minimalist by nature. The following is a list of the items I can't live without.

WINE-OPENERS

There are really only two wine openers that any household needs – a waiter's corkscrew (or 'waiter's friend') and an 'ah-so'. They are each very useful and can be relatively inexpensive.

A waiter's corkscrew is about as basic as it gets. There are variations in shape, but for me the most important element is the hinge. This allows for you to lift the cork straight up, which reduces lateral pressure and results in fewer broken corks. I also prefer a non-serrated blade as teeth can often tear the foil. Having a clean cut on your wine foil is beneficial both aesthetically and from a safety perspective; the foil capsules on a wine bottle can be quite sharp! Nearly a decade off the floor and my right thumb is still faintly striped with scars.

These pictures show how to open a wine bottle using a simple waiter's corkscrew. They also show that the best way to open a bottle which has been sealed with wax is to ignore it and carry on as usual. Just plunge the corkscrew right through and pull up – the wax should break easily.

An ah-so is simply two prongs that, instead of winding through a cork like a screw, hug it from the outside. This is especially helpful with older corks, which are prone to crumbling. If you've never used one before, an ah-so takes a little bit of practice to master, but the steps are relatively simple. Carefully insert the prongs on either side of a cork, then wiggle or 'walk it' downwards using gentle pressure. Once it's all the way in, twist and pull up slowly.

I have opened a staggering number of bottles in my life, and these are the openers I always use. My only addition to this short list would be the Durand, which elegantly combines the standard wine opener with an ah-so. If you find yourself regularly opening older bottles, a Durand might be a worthy investment.

The two images on the left show a bottle being opened with an ah-so. The picture on the right shows a Durand.

AERATING DEVICES

In my opinionated opinion, the only 'aerator' you'll ever need is a decanter. If a wine is so wound up that decanting doesn't cut it – decant it again.

OTHER ITEMS

- **Cheesecloth** Cheesecloth is an inexpensive household item that doubles as an essential wine accessory. If your wine has sediment, or if you break the cork, simply decant your wine through a folded-over piece of cheesecloth. The results should be crystal-clear and free from chunks.

- **Funnel** Serving wine out of a decanter is fine if you are only serving one wine. But if you are opening several bottles, you may want to pour your decanted wine back into the bottle (this is called 'double decanting' and is described fully on page 131). I have tried all sorts of fancy funnels but the best and easiest to use are cheap kitchen funnels made of food grade plastic. Just make sure the spout is small enough to fit inside the neck of a wine bottle without forming a seal.

- **Coravin** This is a big investment for many wine drinkers, but if you find yourself regularly unable to get through a bottle of wine, a Coravin can come in handy. This clever device is outfitted with a slim needle that penetrates the cork, sucks out wine and replaces it with inert argon gas. The remaining wine truly will stay fresh for weeks, even months. It is also helpful if your partner doesn't drink or if you want to compare many bottles of wine outside of a tasting group context.

- **Cradle** A cradle is a somewhat obscure wine gadget that holds a sleeping bottle on its side while you open it. The point of this is to not disturb a wine's sediment. If you don't consume many older bottles, you probably won't need one of these. Should you find yourself wanting to keep a wine prone and don't have a cradle, there are many creative hacks at your disposal. Our cradle broke years ago and since that time we've been lining a salad spinner with a kitchen towel, and it works perfectly.

- **Cloth napkins** While one can technically wipe up a wine drip with a paper towel, a cloth napkin won't leave wet bits of paper clinging where you don't want them. For this reason, I like to keep dedicated wine cloths on hand (sommeliers call them 'serviettes') to clean up messes as I go. Darker colours are better for hiding the stains!

A cradle will help keep a precious or aged bottle of wine prone so you can carry and open it without disturbing the sediment.

WINE SERVICE MADE EASY

R estaurant wine service varies in formality, based on the scope and intention of the dining establishment. Wine service in the home can also range in formality, depending on the vision and bandwidth of the host.

I've been to very elaborate dinner parties with a different wine for every course and a different glass for every wine. The experiences were often grand, but some of my favourite meals were far more casual in execution. Opening a bunch of great bottles, plunking them down in the middle of the table, and instructing everyone to serve themselves can make for a great evening. And it often means the host can actually relax and enjoy the meal.

Your house, your party, your rules.

THE MECHANICS OF OPENING AND POURING

Opening a bottle of wine is not rocket science. Yet there are some professional tips I can give that will hopefully make it easier.

1 Cut the foil under the lower lip. This is both sanitary and practical. If you cut along the top, some wine may collect between the foil and the bottle after the first pour. This encourages drips as well as contamination (some non-toxic but gnarly stuff can grow under the foil if the bottle is old enough). If you accidentally make an unsightly tear, it's best to just rip the whole thing off.

2 Try to get the screw of the corkscrew as close to the centre of the cork as possible.

3 When the cork is mostly out of the bottle, I typically wrap my hand or serviette around it and rock back and forth, with the corkscrew still inside. Then, when it's nearly out, I tilt it at a slight angle to extract the cork as gently as possible.

4 Wipe the inside of the neck with a cloth napkin or serviette before pouring in case bits of cork or sediment are stuck inside.

Pour until the glass is a third full and never touch the bottle to the glass!

5 Pour until the glass is a third full or the wine reaches the widest part of the glass, whichever is less. You want room to swirl and for the aromatics to have space to gather. Never touch the bottle to the glass or you might chip it.

(Depending on how heavily you pour, you could get between five and 10 glasses out of a single bottle; restaurants and bars typically aim for five pours per bottle for by-the-glass offerings.)

6 Right after you pour, give the bottle a little twist of the wrist while lifting. This helps reduce dripping.

7 Be sure to wipe the neck after each pour, or the next attempt will start with a drip.

8 This is a personal decision, but in my house, I always pour a taste for the person who selected or brought the wine (in a restaurant, this would be the 'host') and then go around in a circle from there, filling the host's glass last.

(Though it is the Euro/Western tradition to serve ladies first, I suspect if you asked them, they'd prefer equal pay.)

9 If you are pouring wine while people are seated (especially if a tablecloth is involved), you may want to employ a flexible disc called a 'drip stop'. These aren't particularly elegant looking, but they really do prevent drips. An alternative option is to fill the glasses off to the side and then bring them to the table by hand.

OPENING SPARKLING WINE

Learning the proper way to open sparkling wine is very important. That's because the average bottle contains two to three times as much pressure as a car tyre. Speaking as someone who has shot herself in the neck with a cork, you can really do some damage.

1 **Cutting the foil** Many wine professionals like to cut the foil with the blade of their wine opener, but for me a big part of the charm of sparkling wine is that you don't need any gear to open it. Most sparkling foils have a built-in tab that you can pull, resulting in a fairly clean tear.

2 **Loosen the cage** The single biggest mistake that people, even trained sommeliers, make when opening sparkling wine is removing the cage. DO NOT REMOVE THE CAGE. It should remain attached to the cork at all times. Once you are ready to open the bottle, put your hand or thumb over cork while the cage is still in place and press downward. Only then should you even think about loosening the wires on the cage.

Because it is under so much pressure, sparkling wine is capable of opening itself once the cage has been loosened.

To avoid losing half the bottle in a big splash, you'll want to slow the opening process as much as possible by exerting an opposing force on the cork.

3 **Twist the bottle** With one hand pushing down on the cork and the other gripping the bottle, slowly twist the bottle and cork in different directions. Take care not to point the bottle directly at yourself or others.

4 **Tilt the cork** Once the cork is mostly out, tilt it slightly so that you have a controlled opening. This is not unlike canting the lid of a pot so that a small amount of steam can escape. The ideal sound is a whisper, but if you are looking for a celebratory POP, by all means yank that cork right out. Know, however, that this can turn your bottle into a mini-volcano.

Note *Prior to opening, make sure the bottle is very cold. The warmer it gets, the less soluble the gas, and so pressure increases. You should also avoid shaking or agitating the bottle before popping the cork.*

Sparkling wines are under intense pressure, so using the proper technique to open the bottle is paramount. Always keep your thumb over the cage until the cork is fully extracted.

111

INSIDE TRACK
SABERING

Sabering is a great way to injure yourself while enjoying wine. I've seen bottles 'sabered' with a variety of blunt objects, from picture frames to coffee mugs, but the most common weapon is a dull sword.

Here's how it works. You take a very cold bottle of sparkling wine, remove the foil and cage while leaving the cork in place (remember when I told you never to do this?), and turn the bottle until you locate the lengthwise seam in the glass. You then run the flat end of your sword along the seam until it hits the lip of the bottle. At this point, the top of the neck should break off and a small stream of wine will shoot out. Ideally, the majority of the liquid will remain in your now-decapitated and extremely sharp bottle.

Sabering seems to be gaining in popularity for reasons I cannot fathom. It may be entertaining to watch but the resulting injuries can be gruesome. I've been in the wine industry for over 20 years and have never sabered a bottle. Why? Because I'm smart, clumsy, and no fun whatsoever.

Sabering. Why?

WAX

Opening a bottle of wine that has been sealed with wax is easy. You simply proceed as if the wax is not there. Just estimate where you believe the centre of the cork to be and twist your screw right through. When you start to pull up on the lever, the wax should break off.

The only real complexity enters if a producer has utilized hard wax. Soft wax is fairly pliable, rubber-like, and will break neatly into large chunks. Hard wax, on the other hand, can explode into a cloud of tiny fragments and dust. This stuff is a nightmare to clean and often finds its way into your wine glass. The best option is to hold the bottle over a rubbish bin and chip away at the wax by smacking it with your metal wine corkscrew prior to opening. This will remove the biggest pieces, but inevitably small bits will remain clinging to the neck. I, therefore, usually also tie a cloth napkin around the neck of the bottle before extruding the cork.

Dear producers: please stop using hard wax.

TROUBLESHOOTING DIFFICULT BOTTLES

It always happened at the worst time. I'd be rushing to beat the entrées to a table, a cocktail order still unrelayed to the bar, three other couples trying to flag me down, and the cork would break. In such a moment the harried sommelier has no other choice but to stop, take a deep breath, and *focus*. It is possible, if skilled enough, to wrest even the most difficult cork fragment from the bottle. I fell in love with my husband after watching him extract a hollowed-out cork using the handle of a demi-tasse spoon. But in the home where no one is watching, such wizardry is not required.

BROKEN CORK

If you are at home and the cork breaks, the simplest and best solution is to push the remainder of the cork into the bottle and pour the wine into a decanter (don't forget the cheesecloth!).

I have seen many wine professionals, when facing a broken cork, attempt to remedy the situation with an ah-so. If the top half of the cork is already out of the neck, it's too late for that. An ah-so is best employed when the cork is fully intact. So, if you are opening an older bottle and the cork appears saturated, is squishy or friable to the touch, put the corkscrew down and reach for an ah-so. It should be the first line of defence, not a rescue squad.

SHATTERED CORK

This is a particularly tricky situation. Have you ever attempted to pull out a cork only to have it disintegrate into a pile of sawdust? If that dust falls into the wine, it is very, very hard to remove. The best course of action here is to filter it through a ton of cheesecloth or a very fine mesh sieve. Even so, you may have to repeat this action more than once. Dusty cork fragments ruin the texture of a wine.

FUSED CHAMPAGNE CORK

I have only encountered champagne corks that were fused to the inside of the bottle neck a couple of times in my career, but the memories still haunt me. This typically happens with older champagne, when, for whatever reason, no amount of twisting or pulling will budge the cork. I once had to sneak a bottle into the cloakroom so no one would see me red-faced and sweating, pulling on the cork with all my strength while gripping the bottle between my knees. The only solution I have found for a fused champagne cork is a scary one. You have to use your wine opener like you would for a still wine. Why is this frightening? Because the pressure in the bottle might turn your corkscrew into a weapon. Proceed with extreme caution or just find a different bottle.

PAIRINGS – YOU'RE PROBABLY OVERTHINKING IT

As a sommelier, I loved fussing over food and wine pairings. Finding a dream combination that sets off fireworks inside a guest's mouth and brain is profoundly satisfying work. I truly believe that the right pairing can elevate a dining experience from good to great, or from great to transcendental.

But has the opposite ever happened?

Think about it. Has a wine pairing ever been so bad that it ruined the meal? I've had wine pairings I haven't loved, or might even classify as outright bad, but I still enjoyed myself.

Wine and food pairing is a fairly low-risk proposition. And yet people have so much anxiety over the subject. I personally believe that if you eat what you like, and drink what you like (especially with the people you like), your meal can't help but be delightful.

But for those of you looking for advice instead of a pep talk, here are some simple guidelines. (Note I said guidelines, not rules. There are exceptions to everything below, so please don't let these pointers stress you out. The idea is to have fun and learn as you go).

Finding a dream combination that sets off fireworks inside a guest's mouth and brain is profoundly satisfying work.

1 **Pick a team: wine or food** This is the first and foremost consideration. Are you looking to select a wine to complement an elaborate meal or are you cooking something to flatter a special bottle of wine? Someone needs to lead the dance.

- The nuance and detail of a 40-year-old burgundy might be obscured by an overly complicated dish. Better to prepare a simple roast and let the wine shine.
- On the other hand, a dish featuring dozens of ingredients or a meal with multiple disparate courses is often best served by a high quality but versatile selection (*see* the side box on the facing page).

2 **Match weight and intensity** Ensuring that the wine and your dish are in the same weight class is a reliable way to land on a quality pairing. Roast chicken with a rich Chardonnay is a fine example, as is steak and Cabernet, sashimi and champagne, or Albariño with a fresh green salad.

- Intensity of flavour is important, too. Spicy food with semi-sweet Riesling is a common pairing because sugar is great at softening the bite of especially hot dishes. But an insipid, watery Riesling will get obliterated by a powerful sauce; you want to ensure that your wine has enough concentration and flavour of its own to make a successful match.
- Spicy food also works well with fruit-forward, softly textured red wines. Think Dolcetto, Merlot or a Grenache-based Rhône blend – anything with tons of fruit, limited oak presence and low to medium tannins.

3 **Consider the preparation** Whether a piece of meat or fish is grilled, roasted, steamed or sautéed will change its pairing possibilities. A little bit of char or caramelization often calls for a heavier wine and might skew your selection towards red if you were on the fence.

- The seasoning matters, too. If I'm rubbing a pork tenderloin with chilli powder and paprika, I'm probably reaching for a Zinfandel. If I use garlic and oregano instead, I'm likely going to grab a Semillon or rosé.

4 **Choose a strategy** This is perhaps an oversimplification, but pairings are often classified as either like-with-like or like-with-opposite. Tomato sauce and Chianti is the perfect embodiment of like-with-like; both have high acid and red fruits. And sweet Sauternes with a seared slice of foie gras is the quintessential like-with-opposite. To my palate, matching a sweet wine with something salty like cheese is far better than trying to pair it to a dessert. Sugar on top of sugar can easily be a cloying combination in my opinion.

INSIDE TRACK
DEFINING VERSATILITY

The sad truth is there is no magic wine that tastes great with everything. So if you are stretching a bottle across multiple dishes, a certain degree of compromise is in order. That said, some wines are more versatile than others.

What defines versatility? Effectively, a wine that is neither overly alcoholic, tannic or oaky. This includes such broad categories as lighter reds, rosé, most unoaked whites and sparkling wines. High alcohol wines can interact badly with spicy foods; oak flavours clash with many preparations; and tannin can easily overwhelm light or lean dishes.

WINE QUALITIES AND THEIR DREAM FOODS

Let's assume you are starting your meal planning with a particular bottle of wine in mind. It can be helpful to assess the wine and see if any one element dominates. If so, you may want to use it as a base for your pairing.

TANNIN LOVES FAT

As previously discussed, tannic wines seem to dry out our tongues because the tannins bind to the proteins in our saliva. But tannins will also bind to fat. This is why red wine is so often recommended with meat, especially steak with Cabernet. The fat in the meat makes the wine feel smoother while the tannin in the wine makes the meat taste leaner. And when both the wine and food are elevated, that's an ideal pairing.

ACIDITY LOVES CREAM

Higher acid wines are a sommelier's best friend when it comes to food and wine pairing. When deftly managed, acidity seems to function like salt, enhancing the flavour of a wide range of dishes. It also serves to refresh the palate after a particularly rich bite. Cream-based dishes and fried foods are especially great with high-acid wines. This holds also true for many cheeses.

SWEET LOVES SALT (AND HEAT)

Many consumers consider sweet wines the sole dominion of dessert, but a little sweetness can be useful when pairing with salty or spicy food. We've already discussed the success of an off-dry Riesling with spicy (ie, hot) cuisine, but sweet wine with cheese is another winning combination. Don't forget that sweet

Right It's easy to become overwhelmed when thinking about wine and food pairings, but the risk of mistakes is relatively low.

Higher acid wines are a sommelier's best friend when it comes to food and wine pairing. 99

wines are not uniformly saccharine. There are lightly sweet wines and decadently unctuous ones; always be sure to adjust your pairing accordingly.

GREEN LOVES GREEN

There is a whole class of white grapes that offer a little fleck of green, whether in the aromatics or physical colour of their wines. This list includes Grüner Veltliner, Sauvignon Blanc and Albariño, among others. Dishes composed solely of vegetables, such as salad, are notoriously hard to pair. Look to these bright whites for the best match.

PRO TIP

WHAT GROWS TOGETHER, GOES TOGETHER

If you're an avid home cook who just wants to pick a decent wine without putting too much thought into it, looking into a dish's origin can help. 'What goes together, grows together' is a common trope in the wine industry, though it only refers to dishes that hail from historic wine producing countries (predominately Europe).

People often reference this phrase when discussing the natural compatibility of many high acid Italian reds with tomato-based creations, or wines from Greece's Assyrtiko grape with octopus, or Riesling with schnitzel. It is not a perfect system, but it can often point you in a good direction.

For example, the first time I made choucroute (a particularly heavy dish featuring sausage, sauerkraut and potatoes), I was at a loss for a wine pairing. Then I recalled that it came from the Alsace region of France and tracked down a delicious Sylvaner. The match was perfect.

BEYOND THE TRADITIONAL

Sometimes, the best pairing isn't wine at all.

Though most sommeliers focus on wine, a working knowledge of beer, spirits and cocktails is expected. This is great news for the consumer, especially if they happen to sign up for a tasting menu with pairings. I'm a wine drinker first and foremost, but some of the best pairings I've both created and experienced have been outside of wine. Sake, shochu, mead, beer, *eaux de vie*, spirits and even non-alcoholic creations can make exciting matches. Once, at a José Andrés restaurant, the sommelier mixed a teeny, tiny cocktail for one of my courses. It was delightful.

In my own career, one of my more challenging pairings came early. The chef created a dish that featured seared foie gras (sorry) served on top of a heavily spiced apple sauce. The savoury liver was perfectly complimented by the sugar-and-spice of the apple, but this made for a very difficult pairing. Anything that worked with foie gras (Sauternes, champagne) clashed with the apple. And the best pairings for the apple (dry Riesling, Gamay) fought against the foie gras. After endless auditions, I accidentally stumbled upon the perfect selection: a Belgian white ale. When I approached the table holding a bottle of beer, many guests frowned. But they always smiled after tasting the results.

Once again, the lesson here is: play.

BUBBLES LOVE EVERYTHING, INCLUDING NOTHING

Sparklers are among the most versatile pairing wines out there. They are generally high in acid, and so function like a high acid white, with the bubbles adding an extra sense of refreshment. One of my personal favourite pairings is champagne served with creamy clam chowder. And sparkling wine on its own before a meal is classic for a reason.

SERVING ORDER

Serving order is simply that: the order in which you serve the wines. Given a flight of a single wine style – red Bordeaux, for example – tradition dictates that you would serve the younger vintages first. This reserves the oldest, most complex wines for the grand finale. Similarly, most sommeliers will serve white before red, and lighter wines before heavier wines.

This standard pouring order generally tracks the evolution of a meal, where you might begin with a lighter, vegetable dish and move towards heavier, meat-based selections.

Standard pouring order:

Sparkling wine

Lighter white

Heavier white

Lighter or younger red

Heavier or older red

Dessert wine

For many multi-course meals in the Western tradition, the above works splendidly. But there are other, equally legitimate approaches.

I once worked with an extraordinary sommelier who bucked tradition and insisted on serving the oldest vintages first. His logic was that it was preferable to serve these more subtle, intricate wines when both the palate and the mind were at their freshest. They also tended to be lighter than their younger counterparts, so therefore paired better earlier in the meal. In Burgundy, at least during tastings, it is customary to serve white wines after red. And I personally love to mix things up completely and insert white and sparkling selections in unexpected places. As with everything else in wine, curiosity and creativity can make things a lot more interesting.

GLASSWARE – YOU'RE DEFINITELY OVERTHINKING IT

These days you can find a wine glass for any imaginable category. There are red wine glasses and white wine glasses, Chardonnay glasses and Chianti glasses, 'sommelier' series glasses and stemless glasses, impossibly fragile handblown crystal glasses and chubby but dutiful international standard tasting glasses. You can spend $5 or $50 per stem, invest in one or dozens of options. The possibilities are endless.

So how do you choose?

The first step to making a thoughtful decision is to audit your drinking habits. Do you love to throw elaborate dinner parties with multiple courses featuring all sorts of speciality silverware? You may want to invest in a broad selection of varietally-specific glasses. Do you chug red wine while vacuuming up Lego bricks? Then something sturdier might be in order. Do you spend hours enjoying the bouquet of a rare cuvée? A selection of fine, handblown Austrian stems can enhance your analysis.

It's not a question of which glassware is best. It's about which type of glassware is best for you.

In my house, we historically rely on three main shapes: white, Burgundy and Bordeaux. The following is a rough idea of what we would drink out of each.

The glassware you purchase needs to make sense for your drinking habits and your budget. These are the three basic glass shapes…

Bordeaux:
Full-bodied reds

Burgundy:
Full-bodied whites, lighter-bodied reds, gin and tonic

White:
Lighter-bodied whites, very old reds, sparkling, dessert wine

What guides the shape of these glasses? As evidenced by the hundreds of options on the marketplace, there are a lot of variables at play. But the two main elements are the width of the bowl and the degree of tapering.

A Burgundy glass is named for and designed to enhance the wines of Burgundy – aka, Pinot Noir and Chardonnay. Pinot Noir is notoriously delicate and Chardonnay is not particularly aromatic. The wider bowl allows for a greater surface area of the wine to be in contact with air, thereby coaxing out more of the otherwise reluctant aromatic molecules, and the dramatic taper of the glass effectively gathers and delivers them to your nose.

Meanwhile, the red grapes of Bordeaux – Cabernet Sauvignon, Merlot, Cabernet Franc, etc – are bold with strong aromatic signatures. If you served a Bordeaux in a Burgundy glass, it would appear almost overwhelmingly strong. Such an assertive bouquet doesn't need as much surface area to be in contact with the air, nor any tapering.

In recent years, my household has evolved to favour so-called 'universal' glasses. Many brand portfolios include one in their lineup, and an increasing number of manufacturers specialize exclusively in universal glassware. Such a stem is typically larger than a white wine glass, smaller than a Bordeaux glass, and features a modest taper. These glasses are surprisingly versatile and have the added benefit of taking up less table space while simplifying wine service.

Sceptical? Conduct your own experiment. Try the same wine out of multiple glasses. You might be amazed by the difference.

TEMPERATURE – YOU'RE NOT THINKING ABOUT IT ENOUGH

Hear me out. A wine's serving temperature is just as important as the vessel in which you serve it, if not more.

TAKING CARE OF STEMWARE

It's ok to wash wine glasses in your dishwasher.

Just as with your glass selection, how you handle your stemware needs to make sense for your household. I know several wine professionals that simply throw their – sometimes very delicate! – wine glasses in the dishwasher alongside bowls and cups. Others reserve their stemware for a separate run (no dirty plates), set it to the highest heat, and forgo dish soap. In my house we tend to handwash and have a dedicated sponge just for glasses. This is one area in which we are a little fussier than others.

However you wash them, it's important to dry your wine glasses right away, ideally using a soft, lint-free polishing cloth. If wine glasses dry on their own, water spots form easily. Such marks may appear subtle when the glass is empty but fill it with wine and those spots take on sharp relief. Polishing wine glasses takes a while to master, but it's worth the practice. Note that this is often the point at which a glass is most likely to break, so take care and go slowly.

Where you store your glasses is important too as a smelly old cupboard quickly makes for smelly old glasses.

My biggest pet peeve is restaurants who serve ice cold whites and room temperature reds. A super-cool Sauvignon Blanc might be refreshing on a hot summer day, but over-chilling is not flattering to the wine. At very low temperatures, a wine's aromatics become muted and its flesh feels constricted; only the acidity is amplified.

Red wine has the opposite problem. Served too warm (and 'room temperature' is almost always too warm), a red wine's alcohol and tannins appear elevated and harsh. Though it may run against your better instincts, serving a red with a slight chill will make for a far more compelling glass of wine.

Consider the following. For any given red wine, the winemaker likely blends it at cellar temperature. A sommelier or retailer will then taste it at cellar temperature when considering it for purchase. And a critic will professionally assess it at cellar temperature for review. If you then decide to serve it at room temperature, you are experiencing not only a different wine, but a worse wine.

The following is a list of wine categories and their recommended serving temperatures:

Sparkling or crisp white wines:
7–10°C (45–50°F) (or slightly warmer than fridge temperature)

Full-bodied white wines:
10–15°C (50–60°F) (pull out of fridge half hour before consuming)

Light-bodied red wines:
10–15°C (50–60°F) (aka, cellar temperature, stick in fridge for 45 minutes before consuming if at room temperature)

Full-bodied red wines:
15–18°C (60–65°F) (slightly warmer than cellar temperature)

Dessert wines:
10–13°C (50–55°F) for lighter styles, 10–15°C (50–60°F) for fortified

Personally, I like to start drinking a wine on the colder end of the above ranges, and then let it warm up over the course of dinner. It can be fascinating to mark the wine's transformation as it changes temperature.

Once again, if you are sceptical about my assertions, conduct a home trial. Taste the same wine across different temperatures and decide for yourself whether it makes a difference. Spoiler alert: it does.

DECANTING SIMPLIFIED

First, I'm going to attempt to make decanting as simple as possible. Then I'll explain why it's actually rather complex. Apologies in advance.

There are three reasons to decant a wine:

1 To warm it up
2 To get it off its sediment
3 To give it air

Number one is straightforward. If your red wine is stored at cellar temperature, that may feel too chilly to drink. Decanting is a quick way to increase the temperature by a few degrees.

Number two is also fairly simple. Many red wines throw sediment in the bottle. Sediment is a natural and non-toxic byproduct of wine generally composed of lees (dead yeast cells), tiny grape particles and tartrate crystals. It is most commonly found in older wines, though young unfiltered reds can be quite chunky as well. As previously stated, sediment won't hurt you! But wine is for drinking, not for chewing, so we decant.

If you lack a candle, the torch function on a smart phone will work just as well to help spot the sediment as you decant a wine.

DECANTING FOR SEDIMENT

1 **Make sure you are decanting a well-rested wine**
Sediment needs to have settled for the wine to be successfully drawn off. This is why many people stand bottles up for a day or two prior to opening – gravity forces the sediment to collect at the bottom. If you didn't stand it up in advance and your wine is still resting on its side, you will need to either hold it at an angle when opening or decant using a cradle (*see* picture on page 107).

2 **Open the bottle** Be very careful not to disturb the sediment!

3 **Taste the wine** Tasting the wine prior to decanting is important because if the wine is corked or otherwise irreparably tainted, there is no point in dirtying your decanter. (Pour yourself a sip as gently as possible to not disturb the sediment.)

4 **Position a light underneath** where the neck of the bottle meets the shoulder. A candle is a traditional but the torch on your mobile phone can be easier, won't warm the wine, and does a better job of penetrating dark, thick glass.

5 **Tilt the decanter towards the bottle** You want to run the wine gently down the side of the decanter; holding it at an angle makes this easier.

6 **Pour slowly and avoid glugging** Glugging can introduce unnecessary oxygen and churn up the sediment.

7 **Look for chunks** While pouring, keep your eye on the wine as it approaches the neck. Once you see chunks, stop decanting. Chunks are typically preceded by a fine-grained substance called 'smoke'. Whether or not you let the smoke into the decanter is up to you. Some people insist on a crystal-clear wine and keep it out. Others want to eek as much liquid from the bottle as possible.

8 **Optional: rest and revisit** If the wine is especially goopy, I'll often let the remaining sediment rest in the bottle while I enjoy the contents of the decanter. Then I'll go back for a second, mini-decant to see if another couple tablespoons of wine can be recovered.

DECANTING FOR AIR

On any given day, I get more questions about decanting than probably anything else. Inevitably, people want an easy, one-size-fits-all answer. I always let them down.

Decanting for air is tricky, because I only really know if a wine needs air once I've tasted it. If a wine feels tight, hard, unyielding or ungenerous, I'll decant (I realize this sounds subjective and more than a little vague). Decanting is an area in which experience comes in very handy. If you've had enough Washington Merlots to know what to expect from the category, an unusually stoic one will stick out.

Young reds are most commonly decanted for air, but I find that certain whites, rosés, even the occasional champagne benefit from time in the decanter. Tannic, powerful reds respond especially well, even if they have some age. Pinot Noir rarely needs decanting and anything that tastes oxidized or fragile should never be decanted.

What exactly does decanting do? It softens the rough edges of a wine's texture, emphasizes its fruit and encourages overall harmony. In many senses, decanting acts like a time machine. If you open a wine and realize it's still years away from its peak, decanting gets you at least partway there.

Now that you've determined *what* to decant, *how long* the wine should remain in the decanter is the next question to tackle. I generally decant a wine 30 to 45 minutes prior to consuming it. This is a lot less time than others might recommend but marking the evolution of a wine over the course of dinner is one of my favourite pastimes.

Gauging the ideal duration is a challenge. The more time a wine spends in the decanter, logic dictates, the more generous and harmonious it will become. But it's also possible to push things too far and spoil the wine. This is why I tend to err on the shorter side. If you finish a wine and feel as though it could have benefitted from further decanting, make a mental note for next time. This is a far less disappointing outcome than accidentally driving your wine off a cliff.

Avoid 'glugging' while pouring and tilt your decanter at an angle, so the wine runs gently down the side.

PRO TIP

DECANTING AS A WINDOW INTO AGE-ABILITY

It's hard to accurately predict the lifespan of a wine. But in my experience, behaviour in the decanter can be indicator. Does your wine fall apart after an hour? It's probably time to drink up those bottles. Has it barely budged five hours later? Your wine might still have decades in front of it.

It's worth pointing out that wine professionals don't always agree when it comes to decanting. I once worked for a critic who only wanted to taste and review freshly opened bottles, because that is how most consumers experience wine. Meanwhile, certain winemakers wanted to decant their wines hours in advance, because that is when they felt they show best. It was a constant battle.

CHOOSING THE RIGHT DECANTER

Decanters come in all sizes and shapes, from milk jugs to upside-down mushroom clouds to snakes. As with stemware, the decanter you invest in needs to make sense for your dining habits and your home. If decanting is a rarity in your household or you lack space, you don't need an official decanter at all! In a pinch, any pitcher or other neutral container will suffice.

I primarily use narrow decanters because they are easier to clean and store. These are ideal for older wines because the shape leaves only a small amount of wine in contact with the air. For young, sturdy reds that need to take bigger breaths, a fat-bottomed decanter works best. This shape allows for a maximal interaction between wine and oxygen.

DOUBLE DECANTING, SPLASH DECANTING AND SLOW OX

The method described on pages 127–28 is how most wines should be decanted. But a few other terms pop up from time to time, which I will explain below.

Double-decanting Double-decanting is when you decant a wine, rinse the sediment out of the bottle, then pour the wine back in. It is typically done for practical reasons. If, for example, you need to decant multiple bottles of wine but only own one decanter, double-decanting is essential. Furthermore, some people prefer to serve from the bottle, not the decanter, so that their guests automatically see the identity of the wine without having to ask.

Splash-decanting Splash decanting is exactly what is sounds like. Instead of slowly pouring a wine down the side of a tilted decanter, you tip the bottle upside-down and unceremoniously dump it in. This is usually reserved for *really* tight or *really* young wines (think: freshly bottled).

Slow ox A small subset of connoisseurs will open a wine, remove the cork, and leave it like that for several hours without decanting. This is referred to as 'slow ox' and I typically hear of it being used for old Barolo. I have personally never tried it.

THE FUNDAMENTAL RELATIONSHIP BETWEEN OXYGEN AND WINE

Wine and oxygen have a complex relationship. Oxygen is what catalyzes many of the chemical reactions that contribute to a wine's complexity and maturity. And yet, too much will turn your wine to vinegar.

A significant number of the decisions made during wine's manufacture and enjoyment concern controlling the interface of wine and air. From the shape of the fermentation vessel to the size and newness of the barrels used for ageing, from the bottle closure, to the decanter and stemware. How much oxygen is allowed to interact with the wine, at what time and in what manner, has a profound impact on a wine's final taste.

5

Collecting Wine

For many people, 'collecting' a bottle of wine means hanging onto it for a few days prior to pulling the cork. And that is just fine. Where I'm from, in the United States, there isn't really a culture of cellaring. And many of my more wine-centric friends live in city apartments without room for cases of wine.

But for those who have the space, resources and interest, building a wine collection can be an incredibly rewarding experience. For some, amassing quantities of wine is simply about having ready options at hand. For others, it is a way to explore the transformation of wine as it ages – a bewitching transition that is one of the least understood and most romanticized aspects of wine.

AGEING WINE – HOW WILL I KNOW WHEN TO DRINK IT?

This is a fertile area of insecurity. And for good reason! For many consumers, if they go through the effort of ageing a wine, it's likely because it was either meaningful or expensive. In either case, they want to honour that by opening it at the exact right moment.

But when is the exact right moment?

I get this question all the time and, as with the decanting discussion on pages 129–31, those seeking an easy answer should brace for disappointment. The truth is, there is no one instant of peak maturity, no apex of perfection where all the elements of the wine align in symphonic harmony and kittens and angels and babies come tumbling out of the bottle.

Try letting go of the idea that each wine contains a singular moment of greatness and embrace the thought that each wine contains a plethora of great moments! Hopefully you'll feel some of your anxiety melt away. And when you finally decide to pull that cork, you'll do it with a sense of both confidence and adventure.

WHAT IS THE IDEAL AMOUNT OF AGEING?

The drinking windows appended to tasting notes would have us believe that a wine's ideal age is an objective reality. But beauty lies in the mouth of the beholder.

There is a pervasive idea in the world of wine that older is always better. That's like saying longer books are always superior to shorter ones. I happen to love the autumnal flavours of a well-aged wine, but I recognize that as a personal preference, not a universal one. Many consumers favour the vibrancy of youth, and not because they are ignorant. Critical recommendations in this department should be viewed as guideposts, not gospel.

But what if you don't know your preference? The best way to work out your tolerance for mature flavours is to taste as many older wines as you can. This is not always easy but there are a couple of ways to go about it. You can scour your local restaurants and retailers for back vintages; this can be expensive but has the advantage of instant feedback. Or you can play a longer game and buy your wine in larger quantities.

The latter is something I regularly advise budding collectors. If you fall in love with a wine or taste something special on a trip – purchase more of it than you think you need. Buy at least two bottles, six if you can swing it. Open them at different intervals and note the evolution. Was your last bottle the best of them all? You might like older wines after all. Was it all downhill after the first bottle? Maybe stick to new releases.

But as with everything else in wine: don't make up your mind too fast. Allow yourself the ability to grow and change. Remember, wines aren't the only things that transform as they age; our palates evolve, too.

WHAT HAPPENS TO WINES AS THEY AGE?

This is a subject worthy of its own book, or at least a collection of poetry. For some, the sweetly intricate aroma of a perfectly aged wine is one of life's greatest pleasures. This is why connoisseurs are willing to endure the expense and the risk of chasing old wine, or the patience spent waiting for maturity. For those that appreciate such flavours, the effort is more than justified.

There are some things we know about the transformation that happens during a wine's long slumber, and other things that we only can guess. One thing, however, is for certain: ageing leaves no

A wine is not a banana; what's fresh today will not be bruised tomorrow.

"

stone unturned. Everything about a wine is affected, from its colour to its texture and, most dramatically, to its bouquet.

Visually, white wines darken over time, deepening from gold to brown. Red wines lose colour as pigments drop out of solution, becoming lighter, less opaque and more amber in hue. Fruity and floral aromas are the most fragile and therefore the first to fade. They are eventually surpassed by earthy notes, such as dried leaves, cigar box or incense. White wines often take on more savoury or nutty characteristics. From a textural perspective, red wines undergo the most dramatic evolution, with tannins becoming increasingly soft and smooth. White wines often gain a subtle creamy or waxy feel, dessert wines become less overtly sweet and sparkling wines slowly lose their bubbles.

In the best examples, the overall texture of a wine starts to feel more unified, harmonious. The finish gains in length and the aromatics become increasingly perfumed and heady. At the other end of the spectrum, a poorly ageing wine will become flat, dull, tired and feel as though it is falling apart.

The good news is that, in my experience, wines decline more slowly than people fear. Using Napa Valley Cabernet as an example, the wines tend to hold onto their youth rather tightly for the first decade or so. Then they enter a period of middle age, during which the wine is clearly advancing but still offers plenty of fruit; this can last from 10 to 20 years, depending on the quality of the wine. The wine then enters its final phase of maturity wherein the fruit is but a faded accent and earth-tones dominate, which might last for another decade-plus.

Unless something dramatic happens, like a power outage during a heatwave, an age-worthy wine's transformation is hardly ever sudden. This is why I argue that panic is rarely warranted. If you select wisely (*see* below) and employ proper storage conditions (*see* even further below), stop worrying and leave your wine to its quiet evolution. A wine is not a banana; what's fresh today will not be bruised tomorrow.

WHICH WINES SHOULD I AGE?

Very few wines are intended to age. Each year, the vast majority of wines produced around the world are consumed before the following harvest is even off the vine. So how to know which wines will improve with time in the bottle? It's difficult to predict with accuracy, but I can offer a few guidelines:

Hierarchy helps Because one of the tenets of greatness is age-ability, top-ranked wines have an increased likelihood to improve over time. Think Grand Cru over Premier Cru, a winery's Reserve selection over its entry-level offering, a blue-chip region over an emerging one. There are always exceptions, but this is a solid approach.

Red trumps white Because they have the added protection of tannins, which are both anti-oxidant and anti-microbial, red wines have the advantage when it comes to ageing. This is especially true for highly tannic reds like Cabernet Sauvignon, Nebbiolo and Sangiovese (though Pinot Noir can age with divine grace).

Sweet and sour Dessert wines are among the longest-lived on the planet, especially when buttressed by high acidity. Similarly, high acid whites have the advantage over low acid whites, with white burgundy, Chenin Blanc and Mosel Riesling boasting notoriously long lifespans.

Alcohol preserves Fortified wines such as port, Madeira and some sherries are famous for their ability to age. At high enough levels, alcohol acts as a preservative. This applies primarily to dessert styles, however. High-alcohol table wines that are the result of excessively late picking might have oxidized flavours or diminished acidities and won't typically age well.

Balance over everything In specific contexts, elevated levels of tannin, acid, sugar or alcohol can prolong a wine's life. But if a wine is going to *thrive* in bottle, not just survive, it requires balance. A thin, shrill white might possess abundant acidity, but without the buffering effects of other qualities, it's not going to get better-tasting with time. Craftsmanship, another mysterious and hard-to-measure quality, is also profoundly important.

Let wine surprise you I am a deeply disorganized person. My garage is a crime scene of murdered hobbies, studded with tiny wine fridges. If those refrigerators ever had an order, it devolved long ago. This is how I was able to misplace a mixed case I brought home from a long ago trip to the Loire. Given the opportunity, I would have never deliberately aged a simple white like Muscadet, but I'm glad I did. It's surprisingly wonderful.

In other words, as with everything else in this book, use the above as a guideline, not a rulebook. Many of my favourite moments with wine have been unexpected and unscripted.

> **Many of my favourite moments with wine have been unexpected and unscripted.**

STORING WINE

There is a saying in wine along the lines of: after a certain age, there's no such thing as good wines, only good bottles. This quote highlights the importance of proper storage. It really is the single most important factor in how well a given bottle ages. With lousy storage, even the world's greatest wine doesn't stand a chance of improving in the bottle. But a mediocre wine housed under ideal conditions has at least the potential to become interesting.

In a perfect world, we would all store our wines in a dark space, free from vibrations, at 13°C (55°F), and 75 percent humidity. Of course, not all of us have access to cellars, off-site storage or wine fridges. Because of this, I will offer some practical shortcuts. But before then, I will walk you through and explain the reasoning behind each of wine's preferred cellar conditions.

Laying it down When people say a particular bottle is 'a wine to lay down', they mean it literally. If you are planning to hold on to a wine for even a few weeks, you should age it on its side. This keeps the cork in constant contact with wine, which helps prevent it from drying out. Dry corks tend to shrink, which can let in wine-ruining quantities of air.

Temperature Cryogenics is going to help us all live forever. Why? Because chemical processes slow down at lower temperatures, including those key to the ageing process. This promise is dubious at best for humans but does seem to hold true for wine. Most professionals agree that the ideal temperature for long-term storage is 13°C (55°F); this is often referred to as 'cellar temperature'. That said, 13°C (55°F) is colder than most people enjoy their reds, so many restaurants and collectors set their thermostats closer to 16°C (60°F).

- Temperature stability is another important consideration. As temperatures fluctuate, the wine inside the bottle expands and contracts. This can push against the cork resulting in seepage or a greater influx of oxygen. Both are bad news for wine.

- If you had to choose either a cool temperature or a stable temperature, stability is more important to the long-term health of your wine. That said, long-term storage above 20°C (70°F) is NOT advised.

Light As previously discussed in the Flaws section (page 46), exposure to natural light can be extremely harmful to wine. So please, keep your bottles in the dark or at least behind UV protection.

Humidity Wine lovers keep cellars humid for the same reason they lay bottles down to age – to prevent the corks from drying out. Humidity at 75 percent is the preferred amount because labels and cardboard cases begin to rot at higher levels.

Motion When bottles are exposed to vibrations, like those of a faulty refrigeration unit or regularly passing train, the chemical composition of their contents can be altered in unfavourable ways.

Right Cellars come in all shapes, sizes and designs.

WINE STORAGE HACKS FOR THE CELLAR-LESS

When I first began 'collecting' wine, I lived in a tiny New York City apartment where the landlord controlled the thermostat. I did not have the money to invest in a wine fridge, so I set aside a portion of my closet. This worked perfectly because it was dark, far away from any heating or cooling units (resulting in a more stable temperature), and I was able to stack the bottles on their sides. So, if you do not have access to professional-grade storage, here are your priorities.

Essential:

- Darkness
- Sideways storage
- Stable temperature
- Vibration-free

Bonus:

- Cool temperature
- Humidity

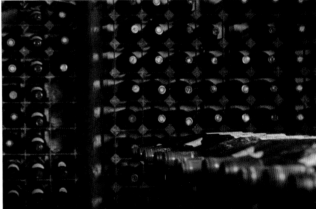

Any place that isn't actively temperature-controlled makes a decent spot to store wine. Garages, wardrobes and stairwells work well, as can under the bed so long as it is far from the air conditioner or heating unit. Lower locations are preferable to higher ones as heat rises. Over the refrigerator or near the oven are out for obvious reasons. Indeed, most of the decorative wine storage racks I see are placed in terrible positions. Unless the bottle is open and you are actively drinking it, the kitchen is probably the worst place to store wine.

THE NON-SCIENCE OF CELLARING

Because of my love of science, I feel compelled to let the reader know that much of the information provided here and elsewhere regarding best cellaring practices is completely anecdotal. The truth of the matter is, we aren't scientifically certain that 55 degrees, 75 percent humidity, and a sideways incline are the best way to store wine. The evidence would certainly indicate this is the case – most of the world's best aged wines were kept under these conditions. But no one's yet conducted a 100-year experiment at various temperatures and humidities to generate actual data on the subject.

That said, there have been a couple of recent studies that specifically call these long-held beliefs into question, but they were relatively short-term in their timeline. One argued that, since the humidity *inside* the bottle is 100 percent – sufficient to keep the cork plush – neither the external humidity nor the orientation of the bottle mattered. Yet another indicated that corks do not, in fact, facilitate oxygen exchange with the outside air: the only oxygen that enters the bottle is that which was contained within the cork cells; a controversial finding to say the least.

These are obviously very interesting experiments worthy of expansion and repetition. So while I freely admit I may one day recant all my storage advice, I'm not prepared to do so until the full might of science overtakes anecdote and experience. For now, I'll continue to play by the old rules.

Think of your fridge as a pitstop, never a parking lot. "

CAN I STORE WINE IN MY REFRIGERATOR?

I highly recommend keeping a couple of bottles of white or sparkling in your fridge for easy access, but only if you plan to drink them within a few months. The fridge is no place for long-term wine storage as it can lead to cork dehydration, even if you lie the bottles on their sides. Some have even suggested that ambient fridge smells can make their way into the wine via the cork (though I have never experienced this myself). If your only other option is a blazing hot countertop, the refrigerator is the better bet. But still, don't let those bottles move in permanently. Think of your fridge as a pitstop, never a parking lot.

HOW LONG DOES A WINE STAY GOOD AFTER OPENING?

Once you pull the cork on a bottle of wine, the clock starts ticking. I generally find most wines stay palatable for a couple more days, depending on the kind of wine. Luckily, there are a few ways to prolong the life of leftovers.

If I can't finish a bottle of wine, be it white or red, I'll jam the cork back in and stick it in the fridge until I'm ready to revisit. The simple act of putting it in the refrigerator, rather than leaving it on the counter, typically buys me at least an extra day since the cool temperatures help slow the oxidation process. Just be sure to let your red wine warm up a bit before you drink it, as overly cold red wine can present itself just as unflatteringly as overly warm red wine.

There are also a couple of relatively lo-fi devices that will suck the air out of an open bottle while sealing it. These might earn you another day or two, on top of what you've already gained by stashing the bottle in the fridge.

Should you continually find yourself unable to get through a whole bottle of wine in a single evening, I strongly suggest either investing in a Coravin (*see* page 107) or looking into half bottles.

STARTING A WINE COLLECTION

Collections come in all shapes and sizes and there's no one perfect way to approach the subject. As with so many things in wine, your strategy (or lack thereof) needs to fit in with your overall lifestyle and budget.

Most of the wine collectors I encounter are omnivorous in their selections. They may buy direct from a handful of wineries, pick up a variety of wines while travelling and purchase larger quantities of wines they've encountered and enjoyed from retailers. The resulting collection is disorganized and completely personal, operating like a kind of vinous diary.

Other collectors specialize right away and focus on a particular region, variety or even producer. This is an interesting approach that, while obviously narrower in scope, allows for a more intimate connection between the consumer and the subject of their affection. I know of one collector who is obsessed with rare German Riesling, Northern Rhône Syrah and Napa Valley Cabernet Sauvignon from the 1970s. He is profoundly well versed on these subjects and would put most scholars to shame. But I'm not sure he's even aware that Italy makes wine.

Once again, there's no 'right' way to build a wine collection. Follow your heart and palate wherever they take you. The only time you need to worry about filling holes in your inventory is if you are sitting on a ton of special occasion wines and don't have anything more casual for pizza night or for when your in-laws drop by. It's also worth saying that you don't need to 'collect' wine at all! Many people simply purchase as needed, storing any given bottle for a few weeks, max. This is a perfectly acceptable way to enjoy wine. But for those who like to stash away a special bottle or two (or more!), some helpful tips are outlined below.

CELLAR MANAGEMENT

Buying a collection of wines is the easy part. Organizing it in a way that is intuitive and simple to maintain is another consideration altogether.

I've seen cellars that are arranged like a small shop, with their inventory divided by country of origin, colour, vintage or even style. These approaches are valid, especially given a large quantity of wine, but I have found that there is one essential category that no cellar should forgo: wines for sharing.

Consider the physical way in which your cellar will be accessed and enjoyed. Are you the only one with a key? If so, organize any way you wish! Are you sharing it with others in your household? Then it's in your best interest to make your system easy to understand, especially when it comes to demarcating communal wine.

Even a small degree of cellar organization will save you time in the long run.

Back in my twenties, when I still had roommates, I scrimped and saved and purchased my first Grand Cru wine – a Chambertin Clos de Bèze from Armand Rousseau (I will not age myself by telling you how much it cost back then, but it was considerably less expensive than it is today). I tucked it away on the wine shelf and practically kissed it goodnight. The plan was to open it in 10 years' time, or when a properly momentous occasion presented itself. So, you can imagine my dismay when I came home one evening to find my roommate, who typically stuck to cocktails, drinking it out of a coffee mug while watching TV. In her defence, I hadn't marked the wine as special in any way; I simply stashed it alongside all the other more pedestrian selections. How was she to know I had serious plans for that bottle?

We want to share our best wines with our loved ones, of course, but we also want to control what and when. This is why I highly suggest setting aside a portion of your collection – and clearly marking it! – for general consumption. In this way, your more precious wines stay safe, and your family doesn't feel anxious every time they reach for a bottle.

Another organizational approach – the one that I employ – is to differentiate not by style or origin, but by drinkability. What I mean is, have one section of your cellar (or one rack in your wine fridge, or pile in your closet) dedicated to early-drinking wine, another for mid-term consumption, and another for long-term storage. Stash that last category in a particularly hard-to-reach place. By keeping the wines I buy for ageing in the most remote corner of my cellar, I reduce the temptation to open them prematurely.

The point is to make things easiest on yourself. What guides your decision-making process in selecting a bottle to drink? Is it age? Colour? Food-compatibility? Price? Whatever it is, make that the organizing principal of your cellar. And then take care to stick to that strategy whenever introducing new wines. That way you don't have to go digging any time you have a specific bottle in mind.

Whether you have 20 bottles or 20,000, a well-managed collection will reduce stress and free up time for the more important things in life. Such as drinking.

"Whether you have 20 bottles or 20,000, a well-managed collection will reduce stress and free up time for the more important things in life.

HIRE A PRO

If you find your collection has reached an unmanageable size, you may want to consider hiring a professional. Many sommeliers or merchants have side hustles tending cellars for private collectors. Services vary but may include buying wine at auction, physically organizing your cellar, conducting regular inventories, providing drinking windows or pairing suggestions, and selling excess stock. They may even host tastings or events in your home.

How do you find someone like this? Ask your favourite sommelier or merchant! The wine industry is small, and there's a good chance they either know someone or know someone who knows someone.

BUYING WINE AT AUCTION

Auctions fall under the category of Advanced Wine Buying. If you are just starting out, I suggest saving this for when you are savvier. If you are really chomping at the bit, you can always lean on a wine professional you trust to guide you through the process. Because while auctions are often the best way to access fine and rare wines (especially older vintages) and to get great deals, there are considerable pit falls. Proceed with caution.

Buying wine at auction can be dangerously fun. The bigger, in-person events often pop corks on some enticing selections from the cellars that are up for sale. This is intended to showcase the quality of the bottles on offer, but it is also meant to loosen the buyers up.

Attendees are typically given a catalogue and a paddle. If possible, request the catalogue in advance and make notes on the wines that interest you. Do this from the quiet of your own home. Take the time to write down the maximum you are willing to spend on a given lot, bearing in mind that you will also have to pay the auction house's premium (a fee that can range from 17 to 25 percent), tax and possibly shipping on top.

Writing down your maximum number before the bidding starts helps maintain self-control. If you are even a little bit competitive, auctions can inspire reckless spending. My husband once spent a bonkers sum on a case of wine because he thought the rival bidder gave him a dirty look. Auctions are madness.

But they can also be a source of incredible value, especially if you bring some specialized and non-mainstream knowledge to the table. During my sommelier days, while paddles were battering the air in a fight over blue-chip burgundy and Bordeaux, I would be quietly snapping up cases of older Spanish and obscure Australian wines for a song.

The explicit origins of an auction's lots are rarely provided. Instead, there is usually a vague description along the lines of 'respected private collector, wines purchased on release and housed in professional storage'. This ambiguity is in place to protect the identity of the sellers, but most auction houses will provide more information if you pick up the phone and call. Similarly, you can sometimes request additional photos or even arrange a private inspection of certain lots.

If the source is ever 'from a restaurant collection', I typically pass. While it does happen that a reputable restaurant closes and liquidates their inventory via auction, I've heard too many stories

Whether I roll the dice on a bottle with a questionable fill generally depends on how little I can get it for.

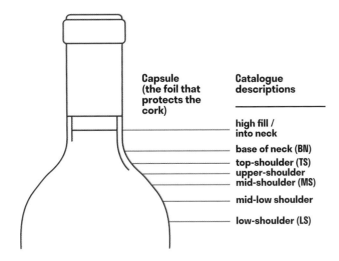

Capsule
(the foil that protects the cork)

Catalogue descriptions
_____

— high fill / into neck

— base of neck (BN)

— top-shoulder (TS)
— upper-shoulder
— mid-shoulder (MS)

— mid-low shoulder

— low-shoulder (LS)

of restaurants dumping their wines at auction following some kind of storage malfunction.

Similarly, I never buy 10 or 11-bottle cases. To me, that indicates the owner opened and tasted a bottle or two before deciding to sell. Perhaps they simply didn't like the wine. Or perhaps there's something wrong with it. Either way, I'm a pass.

Another great way to find bargains at auctions is to bid on bottles with cosmetic flaws. Such wines might sell for a fraction of what a visually perfect bottle goes for, even if the contents are the same. The list on the next page includes some of the more common auction descriptors. The majority denote superficial problems and can be ignored, unless looks are important to you. The ones I pay attention to are ullage and cork conditions. A depressed or protruding cork often indicates poor storage, as does seepage – both are ominous. Ullage (fill level) is a bit trickier. While a shallow fill ought to be alarming and might indicate an issue with the cork, I've had beautiful wines from bottles with shockingly low fills. Whether I roll the dice on a bottle with a questionable fill generally depends on how little I can get it for.

When it comes to buying at auction, your appetite for risk should guide you as much as the above.

This diagram illustrates some of the more common fill levels mentioned in auction descriptions

INSIDE TRACK
A SELECTION OF COMMON AUCTION DESCRIPTORS

ULLAGE, AKA FILL LEVEL (FROM BEST TO WORST):

BN   – base or bottom neck

VTS   – very top shoulder

TS   – top shoulder

MS   – mid-shoulder

LS   – low shoulder

CORK CONDITIONS:

SDC   – slightly depressed cork

DC   – depressed cork

SPC   – slightly protruding cork

PC   – protruding cork

SSOS – slight signs of seepage

SOS   – signs of seepage

WINE LABEL CONDITIONS:

BSL   – bin-soiled label

LL   – loose label

TL   – torn label

STL   – stained label

NOL   – no label

CAPSULE/FOIL CONDITIONS:

CC   – corroded capsule

CUC   – cut capsule

NC   – nicked capsule

NOC   – no capsule

OXC   – oxidized capsule

TC   – torn capsule

PACKAGING NOTES:

OCB   – original cardboard box

OGB   – original gift box

OWC   – original wooden case

WINE AS INVESTMENT

Buying wine for investment is a complicated art. Very few wines appreciate in value and those that do are usually born expensive. This is because it is typically the well-known, established producers from blue-chip regions like Bordeaux, Burgundy and Napa Valley that make good financial investments. Only rarely will an exciting up-and-comer generate significant gains. That said, if you have the resources, the space and the patience, wine can offer great returns.

Selling wine because you have too much of it is not the same thing as investing in wine, even if you make a profit. If you know at the point of purchase that your intention is to never drink the wine but instead flip it, it leads to different behaviours.

First of all, provenance takes on a critical importance, so KEEP THOSE RECEIPTS. If you can prove where and when you purchased your wine, the value goes up significantly. This is especially true if you bought it direct from the producer. Buying direct means the wine travelled once – from them to you, which reduces the risk of in-transit damage. If the wine first went from a producer to an importer to a distributor to a retailer, then it'll be worth less. Similarly, if you buy it at auction, you lose visibility into the chain of ownership.

Secondly, storage counts. It is extremely important to show that the wine has been properly stored while in your care. This is easily proved if you employ a third-party professional facility. If you keep your wines at home, however, the auction house may come and audit your cellar.

Third, buy in quantity and don't touch. Single bottles are nice, and the right ones will sell easily, but the real value lies in full cases, especially if they have never been opened. OWC, or original wooden case, is an auctioneer's dream. Some of the especially big-ticket wines, such as those from Domaine de la Romanée-Conti, come wrapped in metal bands (*see* next page). These are called 'banded cases' and, assuming the band has never been broken, tend to command the highest prices in the after-market.

Fourth, have patience but be vigilant. Investing in wine is like playing the stock market in that you have to know what you are doing – or rely on a knowledgeable pro – to maximize your returns. And while economic swings and currency fluctuations matter to both, wine has the added complication of critical assessment. An older vintage might have a great reputation now, but a negative review by a prominent critic could diminish its value overnight. Also, most wines take a long time to appreciate and yet are perishable physical objects subject to breakage and spoilage. A single earthquake, poorly timed power outage or clumsy uncle is sufficient to ruin even the smartest collection of investment-grade wines.

Finally, explore alternatives. Buying wine to flip is only one way to invest in wines. There are also publicly traded wine companies and wine funds that can represent worthy opportunities.

In short, investing in wine can be both fun and lucrative, but it is not for the faint of heart. Buyers (and sellers) beware.

A banded case tends to bring the greatest returns at auction.

ON GIFTING

I have already stated my belief that there's no greater gift than a bottle of wine, but it's worth revisiting the subject. For those without the time to cook, wine can be the easiest way to contribute to a dinner party. A bottle can express congratulations or condolences, celebrate a milestone birthday or spruce up a mundane Tuesday night. It can welcome new neighbours, honour venerable friendships, seal a deal and toast a farewell – fond or otherwise. And unlike flowers, wine has the ability to improve with age. It can also be regifted if the receiver is not an enthusiast.

Giving someone a bottle of wine is a beautiful way to share something of yourself. Saying, 'I like this, and thought you might like it too' can strengthen the connection between two people, even if you don't end up sharing the bottle together.

The wine you select can tell a story about your own interests and experiences, or it can communicate something you love about the recipient. I recently helped a client select a bottle for their daughter who was graduating from medical school. I steered them towards a Turley Zinfandel, since the proprietor worked as an emergency room doctor for much of his life. I also once arranged for a case of New Zealand wine to be sent in condolence when a client's friend's trip was cancelled due to illness. And when my husband and I got engaged, a dear friend gathered a few bottles from the year we met.

Because wine is made by people, each bottle contains a host of human stories. All you need is a thoughtful merchant, sommelier or writer to hammer the tap.

INSIDE TRACK
BOTTLE FORMATS

Wine bottles not only come in an array of shapes, they come in a range of sizes as well. These vessels have been given all sorts of preposterously biblical names such as Methuselah (six litres) and Salmanazar (nine litres, or the equivalent of an entire case), but the most commonly found alternative formats are half bottles and magnums. A standard wine bottle contains 750 millilitres of wine; a magnum is double that (1.5 litres) and a half bottle is – you guessed it – half (375ml).

Half bottles are handy to keep around if you consistently find yourself unable to finish a whole bottle, but they do age more rapidly so don't stash them away in some dark corner. Magnums, on the other hand, age more slowly than standard wine bottles, which means they retain their youthful fruit for considerably longer. This makes them beloved by collectors and sommeliers alike, but the devil always gets his due – a perfectly aged magnum may provide some of the most exquisite pleasure in the world of wine but it's twice the heartbreak if corked.

Why do half bottles age more rapidly and magnums more slowly than standard bottles? It has to do with the cork. Half bottles, regular bottles and magnums all use effectively the same sized corks (magnum corks are *slightly* larger), which means they all experience the same degree of oxygen exposure, and oxygen is the primary catalyst of ageing. Half bottles age more rapidly because they have half the volume of liquid to contend with all that oxygen; and the opposite is true for magnums.

Note that not all wines come in alternative formats. Many if not most wines are solely available in the standard 750ml size.

6

Understanding Wine

What is wine? And what is fine wine? There are many wine-ish products available on the market today. Wine 'coolers' – made from wine and fruit juice – are a classic from my youth, but there are also cannabis-infused wines, non-alcoholic wines, mulled wines, canned wine spritzers, fruit wines, vermouths, 'clean' wines and on and on and on.

I know many wine professionals who get annoyed at any mention of the above; they prefer a more narrow, 'proper' definition of the term. They want the base material to be solely grapes, they want the alcohol to have derived from fermentation, and they don't want apples or any other foolishness mixed in. Best not to remind them that the Ancient Greeks routinely combined their wines with saltwater, honey and other seasonings before consuming.

I am not overly protective of the word 'wine'. If someone wants to heat-up a mug of spiced Merlot or pour a zero-alcohol grape beverage into a lovely piece of stemware and call it wine, I say 'cheers!'.

But though I will gladly accept – and sometimes reach for – a wine cooler, I tend to drink along more classic lines. I suppose I think of my preferred selections as 'fine wine'. Which, at least in my mind, is a specific subcategory within the broader ocean of wine.

So, what exactly is 'fine wine'? It's hard to say with precision. Fine wine is often discussed in wine media but lacks an official, universal description. Better writers than I have tackled this subject, but consensus has yet to be reached. Some point to wines above a certain price point, or below a certain case count, or made from very specific grapes in very specific ways. But my definition is a bit more emotional.

Fine wine ought to be delicious, of course, but many things are delicious. To be considered 'fine', a wine needs to invoke something more than pure pleasure. Which is why I consider fine wine to be less a luxury good than an agricultural product. One that is authentic to the land in which it was cultivated and the character of its growing cycle. That makes fine wine an artifact of place and time. But in my mind, 'place' is both site and the people that tend it. And 'time' is not just vintage but an era of cultural practices. I liken it to an acupuncturist's needle; fine wine must belong both to the physical point in which it is imbedded and the invisible currents that flow around it.

What does this mean in practical terms? Single vineyard, single vintage wines are obvious candidates for fine wine status. But so are multi-vintage sparkling wines and larger regional blends if they are characterful. I'm even open to more wine-ish creations, so long as they are grounded in a place. But mass-produced wines engineered for maximum consumer appeal simply do not count, tasty though they may be.

Fine wine can't just be made; it must be *grown*.

> **To be considered 'fine', a wine needs to invoke something more than pure pleasure.**

A BRIEF HISTORY OF WINE

It is difficult to say with certainty when humans first began making wine – and each passing year reveals new evidence – but scholars surmise that it likely began during the early Neolithic Era, approximately 7000 BCE. This was the moment in history when we began settling into permanent agricultural communities and contemplating what paired best with mastodon.

Grapes obviously predate wine, and the majority of the world's wine is made from a single species of grapevine: *Vitis vinifera*. Vinifera likely originated in the Caucasus region (the intersection of Europe, Asia and the Middle East – present day Georgia, Armenia and Azerbaijan), but we associate vinifera most closely with Europe. All the wine grapes you know – Pinot Grigio, Cabernet Sauvignon, Zinfandel, Grüner Veltliner, Sangiovese, etc – belong to this species.

In the 9,000 years since the vine was tamed, vinifera has travelled widely. What spurred this expansion? Was early man so enamoured of fine wine's bouquet that he simply couldn't live without it? Yes and no. Through mostly poetic evidence, we know that wine was aesthetically appreciated across written history. But man's relationship with wine has always been more complex than that, and often more utilitarian than romantic.

Religion

Wine's association with Christianity is well-established: Noah's first task upon finding land was planting a vineyard; Jesus' debut miracle was turning water into wine, and modern worship offers a sip of wine as stand-in for the blood of Christ. But wine also plays important roles in Judaism and the religious beliefs of Ancient Egypt, Ancient Rome and Ancient Greece. The expansion of these religions was often accompanied by a spread of viticulture, so that ceremonial wine could be readily produced without the burden of shipping. In relatively recent history, vinifera and the knowledge of winemaking was brought to California by Spanish missionaries in the 1700s, who cultivated vines specifically for the eucharist.

Health

Though today most conversations on wine and health centre around the dangers of overindulgence, wine was historically considered a curative. From the times of Ancient Greece until the early 19th century, the field of medicine was built around what was known as the humoral system. A person's temperament was based on the balance of their various humours (black bile, yellow bile, blood, phlegm) which caused disease if disrupted. Illnesses were often treated with diet, and wine was an important component of that. It was not uncommon for wine to be prescribed for all manner of ailments, but it was believed to bring special vitality to blood.

Wine and other fermented beverages were also consumed for hydration since water was not always deemed safe. Indeed, it would take until the mid-1800s for technology to develop that could reliably supply clean water to cities.

Wine was an important cultural and religious element of multiple ancient civilizations. Here depicted at the Tomb of Ipuy, Egypt, c1279–1213 BCE.

War

Wine's status as a safe alternative to water made it essential to more than one war effort. This is part of the reason Romans spread the vine so far – their soldiers were issued a wine product called '*posca*' (water and wine vinegar) as part of their daily rations. Later, when hydration was not the main concern, the link between wine and war continued, and it was kept around to keep soldiers and sailors happy. The Canary Islands, a convenient refuelling stop between continental Spain and the Americas, were carpeted with vines for this very reason.

Wine's long association with the elite made it a signifier of a 'civilized life' and could imbue the drinker with an imagined moral authority. The wine-soaked Ancient Greeks, for example, looked down upon and derided the Gauls for their beer-drinking ways (I tease my sister similarly). In this way, wine could also function as a weapon of civilization. A number of vineyards and cellars were developed by enslaved or subjugated peoples and wine was also used in the coerced conversion of native populations to Christianity.

Trade

The expansion of wine and the vine followed religious movements and military campaigns, but it also traced trade routes. The Chinese might have been the first to master the art of winemaking, and evidence suggests that it spread along the Silk Road, a trading network that connected much of Asia to Eastern Europe and northern Africa. The Ancient Greeks extended knowledge of viticulture and winemaking around the Mediterranean, the Black Sea and up the Danube in efforts that were part militaristic and part commercial. War between the English and the French in the late 1600s and early 1700s interrupted their wine dealing, which led to the popularization of port. And until the spread of rail systems in the mid-1800s, most wine regions bordered a body of water so that their product could be easily transported for trade. Indeed, part of the historic dominance of Bordeaux, beyond the quality of the wines, was its city's status as an important trading port.

> It was not uncommon for wine to be prescribed for all manner of ailments, but it was believed to bring special vitality to blood.

MAJOR MOMENTS IN WINE HISTORY

In as much as we can say for certain, winemaking seems to have originated in western Asia, travelled to the eastern Mediterranean (western Middle East) and then to Egypt. From there, around 2500 BCE, it spread to Greece by way of Crete. The Greeks, Etruscans and Phoenicians circulated the vine widely. The Romans continued the job, spreading viticulture across much of their empire. Two hundred years after the start of the Common Era, wine grapes were being grown at the north coast of Africa and across most of Europe, including England.

Roman reach made Europe the spiritual and physical heartland of wine production, a position that was solidified after other countries turned away from wine due to religion or politics. But this is not to imply that the European wine scene was either consistent or peaceful after the fall of Rome in 476 CE. What happened thereafter is beyond the scope of this book, but it's safe to say that empires rose and fell, nations settled into their modern shapes and wine traditions formed that were as specific to their respective regions as cuisine and dialect.

The next profound period for wine was Western Europe's colonial expansion, as it spread the wine grape to favourable fields around the globe. This was a time of dramatic cultural terraforming that led to dark days for many, but part of its legacy was the ascendance of dozens of new wine regions across Australasia, Africa and the Americas. These were initially established in the image of Europe but have since evolved their own distinct identities. The first 'New World' vineyards were planted by the Spanish in South and Central America in the 16th century; South Africa was put to vine by the Dutch in the mid-1600s; the British sent vines to Australia in the late 1700s, and North America was then cultivated by the French, English and Spanish during the 17th and 18th centuries.

The Colonial Era saw an unprecedented global exchange of goods. European transplants attempted to recreate their homeland through the importation of plants, animals and cultural traditions; they also sent newly discovered species and ideas back home. This is the way in which the tomato made its way to Italy, the potato to America, and the tea leaf to England – three of the more iconic culinary associations in modern history. But not all the bounty was benevolent; sometime in the mid-1800s, an American pest landed in France that very nearly robbed the world of wine.

Phylloxera is a louse native to the eastern United States that feeds on the roots of vines. American grapevines evolved alongside the bug and are therefore mostly immune, but its effects on the European vine species *Vitis vinifera* are fatal. Within a few decades, the majority of world's vineyards were dead or dying. Eventually, it was discovered that grafting onto American rootstocks solved the problem (the French were not amused!), and today well over 80 percent of global viticulture is based on grafted vines.

Why does this matter? Other than making wine's life flash before its eyes, phylloxera caused a near-total replant of affected regions. This forced a simultaneous worldwide modernization of viticulture.

Prior to phylloxera, new vines were 'planted' by burying the shoot of an existing vine, which would then set its own roots. Over time, this created a complex network of physically interconnected plants. Since grafting requires each vine to have its own discreet root system, this 'layering' practice was abolished. Similarly, vineyards were historically planted as 'field blends', with multiple varieties intermixed that were picked and fermented together. Growers abandoned this in favour of single-variety blocks, which could then be harvested separately at optimal ripeness. These new vines were often planted in rows, which made them easier to access via plough and opened the door to wire trellising and mechanization. Phylloxera also instigated a widespread editing process, with certain varieties being set aside for higher quality or higher yielding cultivars. Underperforming grapevines weren't the only things left on the cutting room floor – entire wine regions disappeared as well, never to return.

Phylloxera's sudden and widespread devastation also caused an acute shortage of wine. Because the initially affected vineyards were French, the first result was a big boost for other countries and regions, such as Rioja and Sicily (Spain and Italy). But the bug eventually reached all corners of Europe, then other continents, and soon the whole world was reeling. Clever criminals took advantage of the chaos and began churning out massive quantities of fraudulent wine and wine products, a practice that continued long after the newly replanted vineyards came back online. Some producers responded by turning to estate-bottling, a rarity until then. And the French government reacted by launching its Appellation d'Origine Contrôlée system in 1935. Known colloquially as the AOC, this then became the blueprint for wine regulation around the world.

The phylloxera louse's full Latin name is Phylloxera vastatrix, *which means 'Phylloxera the destroyer'. These tiny insects live in galls (as pictured* above*) on the plant's leaves and roots and will eventually kill it.*

The above represents some of the most formative moments in wine history. There are, of course, countless others. The French Revolution (1789–99), for example, saw nearly all vineyard land seized from the church and sold to private parties. The advent of the rail system in the mid 1800s allowed inland wine regions to be developed. And then there were the two World Wars, various Prohibitions, the rise and fall of Communism in Eastern Europe, the rise and fall of Apartheid in South Africa, the establishment of the European Union, the emergence of China and India as hot markets for premium wine, the development of social media, the global financial crisis of 2008, Brexit, climate change, COVID-19, tariffs, and so it goes on and on.

Wine's close ties to so many elements of human culture mean it is often profoundly impacted by anything that affects large groups of people. Wine history is human history.

WHAT DOES 'OWN-ROOTED' MEAN?

As previously discussed, the vast majority of wine grapevines (*Vitis vinifera*) are grafted onto American rootstocks. This is because of phylloxera, a subterranean louse that feeds on vine roots in a way that is particularly lethal to vinifera.

Phylloxera has effectively spread worldwide but there are still a few pockets of land either so remote or so forbidding that the pest can't survive there. In such places, vines don't need to be grafted and are planted on their own roots. These are most commonly extremely rocky or sandy sites with very little soil.

Wines made from own-rooted vines are rare and often coveted. Fans believe they are superior to wines made from grafted vines, but this theory is hard to prove as there are few side-by-side examples to compare. In my experience, the wines tend to be very exciting, but that might be because the producers treat them with such reverence. Most scientists and winemakers would argue that grafting has little to no effect on the resulting wine's taste, and that the appeal lies more in their rarity and romance.

An own-rooted vine is simply a vine that has never been grafted.

INSIDE TRACK
WHY DO WINE BOTTLES COME IN DIFFERENT SHAPES?

The four dominant bottle shapes in wine today are the fat-bottomed Burgundy, the tapered Hock form, soldier-like Bordeaux, and the punted, thick-walled Champagne. These shapes have become so indelibly associated with their regions that they have extended to include any associated grape varieties.

What I mean is this. Whether you are purchasing a wine made in Chile or China, a Cabernet Sauvignon, Merlot, Cabernet Franc, Malbec, Sauvignon Blanc or other related variety will almost always be found in a Bordeaux bottle. Similarly, nearly all Pinot Noir and Chardonnay (plus Syrah, Grenache and Gamay from nearby areas) will be in Burgundy bottles. And the majority of Riesling, Gewurztraminer and Sylvaner come in Hock bottles.

In the world beyond France and French varieties, there is a bit more variation. Still, once a region decides on a bottle shape, it tends to stick with it. In Italy, nearly all Nebbiolo comes in Burgundy bottles while Sangiovese wears Bordeaux. Some grape varieties, such as Petite Sirah, hold no allegiances. You can find Petite Sirah in both Bordeaux and Burgundy bottles, but many will choose a Burgundy shape to imply a more elegant style of wine.

In summary, the shape of a bottle of wine is based on tradition with a side of marketing. To the best of my knowledge, it has no effect on the actual taste of the wine.

Burgundy   Hock   Bordeaux   Champagne

OLD WORLD VS NEW WORLD

Part of the reason wine can be so daunting is that, in addition to drawing upon multiple languages, it also possesses a unique vocabulary of its own. There are countless terms specific to wine that can leave new imbibers scratching their heads. Among the many points of confusion are the concepts of 'Old World' and 'New World'.

In wine-speak, Old World means Europe and New World refers to everything else, from South Africa to New Zealand to Canada. Historically, the line between these two 'worlds' was not only geographic and historic, but also stylistic and regulatory. And while dividing global wine production into two camps could be occasionally useful, the distinctions are arguably less meaningful than they used to be. I'll address each of them below.

History

From an historical perspective, the word 'new' is a bit insufficient. Though they certainly can't compete against Europe's millennia, South America and South Africa's wine industries date back to the 1500s and 1600s, respectively. Even California, which only really hit its stride in the mid-1800s, is hardly a babe in the woods.

Furthermore, what about wine regions that pre-date Europe? I'm speaking specifically of places like Lebanon, Armenia, Egypt, Turkey, Georgia and even Greece, which only joined the EU in 1981. Though these countries occasionally get lumped into a lesser known third category called the 'Ancient World', they certainly challenge Europe's primacy over all things old.

Style

For most of my 20-plus year career, the stereotype was that European wines were more elegant, lower in alcohol and

Parmesan is not just a cheese; it is an edible hunk of culture. The same is true for wine.

occasionally earthier than their New World counterparts. And while one needed only look to Châteauneuf-du-Pape or Priorat to know this wasn't *always* true, nine times out of 10 it felt accurate. But today, with the triple forces of improvements in farming, shifting consumer preferences and climate change, it's harder to generalize. These days, it is just as easy to find a truly ethereal New World wine as it is to locate a densely concentrated and lusciously ripe European wine.

Regulations

When asked about the differences between Old and New World wines, I always say the same thing. From the perspective of consumer engagement, the primary distinction is that New World wines tend to lead with the grape variety, whereas the Old World focuses on place. You almost never see the grape listed on a bottle of European wine. It is up to the consumer to know that Meursault is always Chardonnay, Savennières is always Chenin Blanc and Rioja is predominately Tempranillo.

The reason that Europe tends to label according to place is a matter of mindset. It sees wine as a key element of a region's cultural heritage, which is also why there are so many regulations in place that codify and preserve a given wine's traditional methods of manufacture.

If, for example, you own land in one of the Barolo DOCG subzones of Piemonte and want to label your wine as such, there are restrictions as to what you can grow, the ripeness at which you can pick, how long you can age your wine, the number of vines per acre and the amount of fruit you can harvest. Even the permitted elevation and orientation of your vineyard is regulated (due north is not allowed!).

This place-forward mentality extends to other goods as well. Cheese is an obvious parallel. Parmesan can't be made in any part of Italy and from any type of milk. It must be produced from certain villages in Emilia-Romagna and Lombardy, from cow's milk, according to very specific methods. This level of oversight ensures that once the Parmesan leaves Italy and ventures out in the world, it will offer an accurate reflection of its place of origin. Parmesan is not just a cheese; it is an edible hunk of culture. The same is true for wine.

This is not to say that non-European producers don't take their wines, regions or cultures as seriously – many do. It's simply that the New World doesn't experience the degree of oversight or approach wine labels in the same way.

TERROIR AND 'WINES OF PLACE'

I'll never forget my first trip to France. It was the summer after my sophomore year of college, I was 19 years old, and I was freaking out. At this point in my life, I had barely set foot in a museum and never even tasted wine. I selected Paris as a destination because I had a friend living there at the time and also, well, because it was Paris.

This was back when flying was still a fairly luxurious experience, even if you bought the cheap tickets. Nonetheless, it took all my money to get there. I landed at Charles de Gaulle airport and, straining to recall my high school French, made my way to the train. The ride to downtown Paris is long and dull, which only increased my anticipation. At some point, I emerged into the hot summer air, ready to witness Paris in all her glory. What I saw instead was a Gap.

I had flown across an entire ocean to be greeted by an American chain retailer.

Terroir is one of those tricky wine words that new drinkers struggle to comprehend. It's effectively a non-translatable French term that describes the distinct character of a site.

Terroir is commonly believed to encompass a vineyard's terrain (soil, slope, elevation) in addition to its microclimate. Contemporary thinking has expanded this notion to include a vineyard's microbiome – the yeast, bacteria and fungi present both above and below ground. Some even believe that humans are an essential element of terroir; that you cannot treat man's presence or his farming decisions as independent from site expression.

In other words, a vineyard's terroir is its voice. It is the unique combination of attributes that make wine from one place different from another. And wines that emphasize their terroir are often referred to 'wines of place'.

Of course, not all wines seek to express their origin. Some are big juicy blends engineered for style and consistency. But more and more, at least in geeky circles, the prevailing idea is that site expression is the highest and best duty of a wine.

My theory is that globalization has pushed this particular narrative. That, in a world paved

Vineyards come in all shapes and sizes, but they differ in unseen ways as well, such as microclimate and the soil's microbiome.

A vineyard's terroir is its voice. It is the unique combination of attributes that make wine from one place different from another.

in smart phones and studded with Starbucks, authenticity has become fetishized. In wine terms, this has resulted in an almost over-emphasis on site-specific wines, with primacy given to single vineyards or, better yet, single blocks within vineyards.

This leads to an interesting philosophical debate about place. How small must a place be to be considered distinctive? How large might it be? At what scope does the concept of place become meaningless? Gevrey-Chambertin is a place, and a quite characterful one at that. As an appellation, its wines are distinct from nearby Chambolle-Musigny. Is its place-ness somehow less valid because it is significantly larger than the single-vineyard sites it contains?

I'm a true terroir-believer and my favourite wines reflect their place of origin. But I'm also wary of the industry's obsession with the small and the scarce. A single vineyard wine is not always better than an appellation wine, which is not always better than a regional wine. And not every declared vineyard is worthy of special attention.

As always, keep an open mind while tasting and rely on your own judgement. Great wines can hide in unexpected places.

7

Making Wine

Every autumn in Sweden, a drunk moose stumbles into town and raises hell.

How did the moose become inebriated? By eating apples that had fallen onto the ground and fermented. Yeast, naturally present on the skin, made its way into the flesh via a hole or a split and set to work converting the apple's natural sugar into alcohol. The result would technically be considered cider. The same phenomenon happens with grapes and birds all the time; robins love a sip or two of wine on a crisp fall afternoon; thrushes are notorious lushes.

Fermentation is as old as fruit and just as natural, but it is only one small step on the journey from vine to glass. There are infinite other factors a winemaker must consider when crafting man's most mystifying intoxicant.

THE ART OF WINEMAKING

Winemaking involves formidable skill and scientific know-how. There's the biology of microorganisms to consider, their population dynamics and nutritional requirements. The thermodynamics of fermentation is another point of concern and touches upon the world of physics. Chemistry abounds, from pH shifts in acidity to redox reactions and the conversation of sugar into alcohol. And then there is the sensory evaluation that takes place at every stage, for sometimes the best warning that things are about to go awry is a single disconcerting whiff.

Winemakers are craftsmen, scientists, mechanics and sometimes farmers rolled into one. But the best of them are also artists.

Wine is an unnatural stopping place between fruit juice and vinegar. Though it is hewn from nature, it is very much a man-made product. As such, the final taste of the wine is owed, at least in part, to the talent and inspiration of the person who tended it. The finest wines I've enjoyed inevitably came from great sites. But they were also crafted by people possessed of remarkable creativity and sensitivity.

The strategies employed by such a winemaker are often intuitive and not easily itemized. So, I am going to skip the art part and focus instead on the craft. The forthcoming sections detail the basic steps most winemakers undertake when producing a solid bottle of wine. Needless to say, there are infinite variations, and specific practices vary according to grape variety, climate and intended style. But my hope is that the following information will provide useful insight into the physical act of winemaking.

> **The finest wines I've enjoyed inevitably came from great sites. But they were also crafted by people possessed of remarkable creativity and sensitivity.**

RED WINE PRODUCTION

Squeeze almost any red wine grape and the juice will be clear. So how does red wine get its colour? By macerating with the skins! The skin of a grape is where all the colour and most of the tannin is located. This is the reason why white wine has (mostly) neither colour nor tannin – because winemakers press the fruit right away and discard the skins.

PROCESSING THE FRUIT

Harvest

Red wine grapes are harvested when the winemaker determines that the perfect balance has been struck between the amount of sugar, the level of acidity, the quantity and ripeness of the tannins and the complexity of the flavours. That, or a storm is coming.

How early or late a winemaker picks can influence the final style of the wine. Wine from early-harvested fruit will usually be higher in acidity and lower in alcohol, with brighter flavours. Wine made from later-harvested fruit will often be fuller-bodied, higher in alcohol and lower in acidity with softer tannins and darker flavours.

Destemming

Grape clusters can be either destemmed or left intact. If destemmed, the berries are often gently cracked so that their juice can easily escape. If the clusters are not destemmed and the berries remain whole, the fruit might be intended for carbonic maceration (*see* page 180). (Fetishists take note: this 'cracking' of the fruit was historically done via the human foot! And, in some places, it still is.)

Sorting

Quality-minded producers often engage in some degree of sorting, whether it's by cluster or by berry. Fruit might be rejected if it is underripe, overripe, rotten or damaged. Material other than grapes (MOG) such as leaves, sticks and salamanders are also removed at this point.

Maceration

Colour and tannin are mostly extracted during the churning heat of fermentation, but some producers like a little extra oomph. Pre-fermentation maceration is also referred to as a 'cold soak'. Because it happens before any alcohol is produced, it's a gentler process and tends to extract more colour than tannin. 'Extended maceration' happens once fermentation is complete and is often used to encourage tannins to knit together into smoother-feeling configurations.

How much maceration a wine experiences can influence its style. Heavily macerated wines tend to be darker and denser than those that spent a shorter time on the skins. Think of it like a cup of tea – the longer you leave the bag in, the stronger the brew.

MANAGING FERMENTATION

Choosing a vessel

Fermentation can take place in all sorts of vessels, from massive tanks to tiny barrels. The shape, size and material of the tank all leave a lasting imprint on the wine. High-quality producers tend to use smaller vessels in order to focus on specific vineyard parcels. Stainless steel tends to emphasize fruit, wood is often used to soften tannins, and concrete and clay can enhance minerality.

Yeast

A producer can choose to inoculate with commercial yeast or to rely on naturally present ambient yeast. Commercial yeast offers greater control and a more predictable fermentation process, but many argue that embracing local ambient yeast results in greater complexity and site specificity.

Temperature

Red wines are generally fermented at higher temperatures than whites, as this enables an easier extraction of colour and tannin. The typical fermentation range for red wine is 24–35°C (75–95°F). Note that while many tanks are temperature controlled, fermentations generate their own heat as part of the chemical transformation of sugar into alcohol. Carbon dioxide is another byproduct of fermentation.

Pumping over/punching down

There are many reasons to keep wine circulating in a tank. It introduces oxygen, which helps the yeast do their work, ensures an even fermentation and enhances extraction. It also prevents the drying-out or rotting of a tank's 'cap' – a collection of grape skins pushed to the surface via carbon dioxide. To ensure the cap stays wet, a winemaker can either pump over (mechanically move wine from the bottom of the tank to the top) or punch down (manually use a plunger or other device to submerge the cap). Pumping over or punching down typically occurs one to three times a day for the duration of fermentation.

Pressing

Once a fermentation is finished, a winemaker will want to drain the wine from the tank and press the leftover solids. Though most of the berries will have emptied during fermentation, there is usually still some yummy stuff hiding in the leftover fruit. Pressing releases this slightly sweet and flavourful juice, which is often kept separate, though it may be added back in during blending.

Quality-minded producers typically press on the gentler side, as harsh compounds can be released at high pressure, including bitter tannins from grape seeds. Wineries pursuing a more elegant style may not use the press juice at all.

Winemakers have a range of fermentation vessels to choose from, and their selections may be guided by style, budget or logistics.

ELEVAGE

The French term '*élevage*' translates as 'to raise', as in rear a child. It refers to everything that happens to the wine between pressing and bottling.

Barrels

Once a tank is drained and the fruit solids pressed, the resulting wine is often aged in barrel. And as with tanks, the size, shape and composition of a barrel will have an impact on the final wine. Barrels are the vessel of choice for red wine because they are porous. They allow a small amount of oxygen into the wine, which helps smooth the tannins and integrate flavours.

- The newer the barrel, the more oak flavour it will impart to the wine.
- The smaller the barrel, the more oak flavour it will impart to the wine.
- Newer barrels tend to have larger, unclogged pores and therefore allow for a greater influx of oxygen. This is why you tend to see a higher percentage of new oak used with tannic varieties like Cabernet Sauvignon – the oxygen helps the tannins resolve and feel more smooth.
- Barrels can be made from many different types of wood, though oak is most common. The precise qualities of the oak differ according to species, country of origin and even forest of origin – Allier and Limousin are examples of French oak forests.
- Barrels are typically bent into shape via fire, and the amount of char left inside the barrel also impacts the final expression of the wine, with high char contributing dark and toasty aromas.

Ageing

The length of time a wine spends in barrel has to do with the grape variety and style of the wine; tannic varieties like Tempranillo benefit from extended ageing while more elegant wines such as Pinot Noir tend to enjoy a shorter period of ageing. In Europe, the length of time in barrel is often dictated by a wine's appellation regulations.

Racking

A barrel's pores let in a small amount of oxygen, but sometimes more is necessary. A wine is 'racked' when it is drained from its barrel and moved into a different barrel. This helps keep the wine healthy (certain varieties get stinky if they don't get enough early access to air) but can also be a way to remove any lingering solids from a wine, which tend to settle out during the ageing process.

Blending

Many people think 'blending' only happens when you mix two different grape varieties together, such as Syrah and Grenache. But almost every wine is 'blended' in some capacity. Different barrels, lots and vineyard plots might contribute different qualities to a mix and some might be excluded from the blend altogether.

Fining/Filtering

If you've ever noticed sludge or chunks in your glass, you know that wine is not purely liquid. There is a considerable quantity of suspended solids in wine, including yeast cells and bacteria, tannin and pigment molecules that have come out of solution and tiny bits of grape skin. Fining or filtering can remove these materials, with fining considered the less intrusive method.

- The classic example of fining is using egg whites to strip excess tannin from Bordeaux. A cellar worker will crack fresh eggs, separate and stir in the whites, and wait. The protein in the egg binds to the tannin in the wine and removes it from solution.
- Fining and filtering can improve a wine, but they can also remove flavour, if poorly executed. Because of this, some wines proudly advertise that they are 'unfined and unfiltered'.

INSIDE TRACK
AMBIENT YEAST

The world contains approximately 1,500 different species of yeast but only a very small portion of these is appropriate for winemaking. In order to ferment wine, a yeast has to like the sugars on offer and be able to withstand the presence of alcohol, acid and heat. Saccharomyces checks all these boxes and therefore is the dominant wine yeast strain, but a handful of others can happily contribute to fermentation if given the chance, including some pesky spoilage yeasts.

Yeasts are omnipresent and can be found on many surfaces, including grape skins and the inside of wineries. For thousands of years, people relied on these invisible agents to make wine without even knowing they existed. Their identity was first revealed in the 1680s, but it would take another 200 years to confirm their role in wine.

Dried, pre-prepared yeast wasn't available commercially until 1965 but it didn't take long for it to become a fixture of modern winemaking. Adding yeast gave the winemaker greater control. Not only could they reliably avoid

A NOTE ON ADJUSTING ALCOHOL LEVELS

Though it's hardly a popular topic among producers, winemakers all over the world adjust alcohol levels in both red and white wines, and not infrequently. This can be done via several different methods.

In Europe, it is illegal to add water to a fermentation to reduce the alcohol, but adding sugar is permitted in some places to increase it. This process is called chaptalization and it is more commonly employed in cool regions where the climate has traditionally not been warm enough to achieve full ripeness in the grapes. When done well, a small amount of sugar is added early in the stalled or spoiled fermentations by using specialist yeasts, but eventually they could customize their selections to enhance or add certain aromatic qualities.

But like all fashions, once designer yeast became associated with mainstream winemaking, it inspired a revolt. Winemakers began to revisit the idea of ambient fermentations (though it's worth saying that many never utilized commercial yeast in the first place). This has happened across all levels of the quality spectrum, though mass-produced wines are likely still made exclusively via inoculation of pre-prepared yeast.

Recently, the swelling interest in ambient (often referred to as 'native', 'wild' or 'indigenous') yeast has run parallel to a rising interest in site specificity. The thought is that ambient yeast will not only provide more complexity than a single commercial strain but will also better reflect the unique characteristics of a given vineyard. Faced with the opportunity to tap more deeply into terroir, some producers are happy to accept the risk, however small, of a difficult fermentation.

fermentation process to bump up the alcohol level slightly and round out the texture of a wine. Rules regarding chaptalization vary from country to country and region to region.

In hotter regions outside Europe, it is not uncommon for the winemaker to lower potential alcohol levels by adding water to a fermentation. Some producers will go a step further and remove alcohol using a centrifuge in a process called de-alc'ing. Both of these practices are somewhat controversial yet are rarely obvious to the consumer tasting the wine in the glass.

PRO TIP
WHOLE CLUSTER FERMENTATION

There are three main reasons to employ whole clusters (aka non-destemmed, non-crushed berries) in red wine making: for stem inclusion, for carbonic maceration or for both.

Why would a winemaker deliberately include stems? And what is carbonic maceration? The answers are below.

Stem inclusion

In California, where I live, it is not an uncommon site to see a winemaker sunk legs-deep in a tank, diligently treading on a layer of whole grape clusters. Their feet break open the berries, releasing the juice, which will then macerate with both skins and stems alike. This process is thought to add complexity (stems can contribute a subtle herbal or savoury tone as well as a tickle of tannins), to increase the sensation of freshness (stems can absorb small amounts of alcohol), and to naturally reduce the fermentation temperature. As underripe stems can be overly green tasting, only darker or more lignified stems are typically included.

Carbonic maceration

This is a bit technical so bear with me. Carbonic maceration happens when an intact berry begins to ferment on its own. This is instigated not by yeast but by enzymes naturally present in the grape. The result is a subtly different flavour profile than that given by traditional fermentation. Berries are only able to ferment up to 2% alcohol this way, however, so eventually need to be crushed and fermented normally. A wine that has experienced carbonic maceration tends to be lighter, fruitier and more floral. Beaujolais Nouveau is the classic example, but many other wines employ some degree of carbonic maceration.

Above *Whole clusters destined for carbonic maceration.*
Below *Destemmed berries on a sorting table.*

Using both stems and carbonic maceration

When a winemaker uses whole clusters – even if they tread the fruit thoroughly – some berries will likely remain intact. This marries the aromatic complexity and fuzzy grip of stem inclusion with the bounce and charm of carbonic maceration. It is not uncommon to hear a winemaker speaking in percentages, as in: 'I used 25 percent whole cluster on this wine.' What that means is they destemmed 75 percent of their fruit and left the remaining quarter as whole bunches.

INSIDE TRACK
WHAT IS VINTAGE VARIATION?

Vintage variation is the natural deviation in a wine's expression due to changes in weather from one year to the next. Magazines will often describe a year as 'good', 'bad', or maybe even 'great' but there is considerably more nuance involved in assessing the annual wine crop.

Some outcomes are obvious, such as a hotter vintage will yield fuller, softer wines. Or that a cooler year might bring out a more austere expression, with higher acidity and lower alcohol. Or that rain at harvest might result in dilute flavours. But vintage characteristics are not always so easily explained. What about such intangible attributes as 'balance', 'concentration' and 'character'? These also vary from year to year.

Much of a vintage's quality is written in the weather, but the vineyard plays a role as well. To a certain extent, vines have a mind of their own. For example, if a frost slashes yields, the vines might respond by setting a massive crop the following year. And even if the weather is uncommonly beautiful, the farmer might be unable to coax greatness from an overly vigorous year, despite his best efforts.

Finally, how does vintage variation square with site expression? If, as we're taught to believe, the best vineyards have a specific voice that rings out through its wines, how can we accept that it changes from year to year?

I like to think that a vineyard's voice remains the same, but the pitch changes. Or perhaps it's the message that shifts. Some years, the vineyard states something profound; other times it whispers, or perhaps just passes the time with charming small talk. We also vacillate, and these moods are often shaped by outside forces. Vines are no different.

WHITE WINE PRODUCTION

Compared to red winemaking, white winemaking is relatively simple; but there is also less room for error. Because red wines have all that concentration, pigment, tannin and sometimes oak to distract us, they can more easily hide blemishes; there's simply more 'noise' with red wine. Great white winemaking, on the other hand, is an exercise in precision.

PROCESSING THE FRUIT

Harvest

Since tannins are not really a consideration with white wine, the winemaker tends to focus on the balance between acidity and sugar, as well as the complexity and concentration of flavour. It can be argued that choosing the exact right date of harvest is more important for whites than reds.

Sorting

The fruit for white wine is generally sorted by cluster. White grapes are pressed and macerated quickly, so rarely need destemming.

Some years, the vineyard states something profound; other times it whispers, or perhaps just passes the time with charming small talk.

Pressing

The primary difference between white and red wine is that, with white wine, the pressing happens right away. Sometimes the juice is left in contact with the skins for a few hours to extract a little extra colour and flavour, but that varies by producer. It is also common for white wine to undergo far gentler pressing than red.

Settling

Even the most well-tended fruit is covered in dust and other detritus when it arrives in the winery. Because of this, white wine makers will often 'settle' the juice overnight, and then drain the clear liquid off the solids at the bottom of the tank prior to fermentation.

MANAGING FERMENTATION

Choosing a vessel

Because white wine fermentation doesn't involve any pesky grape skins or seeds, there is a greater flexibility in terms of vessel. Stainless steel is popular for its tendency to preserve fresh fruit flavours and because it can be easily temperature controlled. Chardonnay and other white varieties such as Chenin Blanc might be fermented in barrels. This can add textural richness to a wine and may also impart oaky notes if the barrels are on the newer side. Alternative vessels, such as concrete eggs or clay amphora, can also be employed and are thought to emphasize minerality and purity.

Temperature

White wines tend to be fermented at lower temperatures than red wines. This helps preserve the more delicate fruity and floral aromatics, which are key to many white wines. The common range is 7–18°C (45–65°F), with barrel fermentations (which cannot be temp-controlled) hitting as high as 27°C (80°F).

ELEVAGE

Barrelling down

When a white wine's fermentation is completed, the winemaker has the option of bottling it or 'barrelling down'. This is the act of dividing the wine into barrels for longer ageing. Oak barrels are most common, though stainless steel are becoming increasingly commonplace.

Stirring

When a wine is ageing in the cellar, a winemaker might elect to take the time to stir each individual barrel. The French call this *bâtonnage*, and it helps build texture in the wine by introducing oxygen and circulating the lees (dead yeast cells and other particulate matter).

Malolactic fermentation

Malolactic fermentation (MLF) is a process in which bacteria convert malic acid to (softer) lactic acid. What this means in layman's terms is that the wine's perceived acidity drops. Nearly all red wines undergo MLF but with white wines it is a stylistic decision. If, for example, you are making Chardonnay from a warm site and wish to preserve acidity, you might block MLF.

Ageing

On average, white wines spend less time in barrel than reds. Even the oakiest white tends to be bottled prior to the subsequent harvest, though there are always exceptions.

Filtration and stabilization

Consumers may tolerate a little sediment in their red wines, but most people expect their white wines to be completely free from solids. Because of this, whites are commonly filtered or at least cold-stabilized, which prevents the formation of small crystals. Though harmless, these crystals bear a frightening resemblance to broken glass and their presence has caused more than one bottle to be returned.

ROSÉ AND ORANGE WINE PRODUCTION

As previously discussed on pages 21–22, rosé can be made in several ways.

In the classic style of Provence, whole clusters of red grapes are harvested and pressed, with the juice kept on the skins for a couple of hours – just long enough to impart a pale hue to the wine. Knowing that the fruit is intended for rosé changes the way the vines are farmed and when the fruit is harvested. Grapes destined for rosé are often harvested from high-yielding vines whose fruit is less likely to be overly concentrated (concentration is not a desirable quality in most rosé), and harvest is typically earlier, resulting in higher acidity and lower alcohol. Elegant Provençal rosés will likely be fermented in stainless steel and bottled shortly after fermentation. Occasionally, some rosés are barrel-aged, but that is rare.

The other prevalent way to make rosé is via the *saignée* method, wherein a tank of newly fermenting red is drained of some of its juice. Saignée rosés tend to be darker pink than the Provence-style, with slightly higher alcohols and riper flavours. This is largely because the fruit was harvested according to red wine standards, which favours tannin maturity. As with the Provence style, these wines are often fermented in stainless steel and bottled shortly after fermentation.

There are other, more obscure ways to make rosé. In Champagne, a small amount of still red wine can be added to a clear sparkling base. In other parts of the world, white and red grapes might be fermented together, resulting in a lighter style of red wine that can be quite rosé-esque. This is an ancient style of winemaking that is making a tiny comeback, though it is still quite fringe.

Orange wine results when white grapes are processed as if they are red. Which is to say, the grape skins are kept in the tank during fermentation. There is so little orange wine made relative to other categories that it is difficult to generalize about winemaking techniques. I know some producers that ferment their orange wine in stainless steel and age it in oak barrels – similar to classic modern red winemaking. Others might ferment and age their orange wine exclusively in clay amphora. The category really varies.

One note I'd like to make is that some orange wine producers, especially those that identify with the natural wine movement (which emphasizes minimal manipulation), may deliberately refrain from filtering or cold-stabilizing their wines. Because of this, some orange wines may appear hazy or even throw a sediment. This is completely normal and harmless to consume but can be alarming to those reared on the twinkling clarity of mainstream white wines.

SPARKLING WINE PRODUCTION

Sparkling wine is on fire. Its category has experienced profound growth over the past few decades. Suddenly, it feels as if sparkling wines are being made in every possible region, and via every imaginable grape. This is great news! Nothing is more joyful than bubbles and these days, the world needs as much joy as it can swallow.

At the high end, established brands and the classic wine regions are making better wine than ever before. The changes that have befallen Champagne, specifically the rise of smaller brands known as grower-producers (*see* page 194) and an increasing interest in sustainable farming practices, have been a boon for the region. Sekt, Cava, Prosecco and Franciacorta (the sparkling wines of Germany, Spain and Italy) have responded to the swelling demand with huge jumps in quality. And elsewhere, but especially in the New World, producers are experimenting with new styles of sparkling wine, many of which abound with playfulness and creativity.

I recently tried a Napa Valley sparkling wine made from 100-year-old French Colombard and Chenin Blanc vines. It was delightful! And it made me wonder: is the sense of freedom embodied by many in the new wave of sparkling wine a reaction against the establishment or a continuation of Champagne's legacy? After all, champagne is itself rather unusual in the context of modern Europe, being one of the few classic wines that blends across vintages. It also routinely combines red and white grapes together. Many imagine Champagne and its wines as established, grand and traditional. But viewed in a certain light, they can appear rather radical.

THE CHAMPAGNE METHOD

There are many ways to produce sparkling wine but the most esteemed (and labour intensive) belongs to Champagne. Because the wines are so highly regarded, the Champagne process is mimicked by wineries all over the world. If a producer elects to make their sparkling wine in this manner, it is typically advertised on the wine label as 'traditional method', '*méthode traditionelle*', '*método tradicional*' or '*metodo classico*'. The steps are detailed below.

Note *Not all French sparkling wine is champagne. To be called champagne, the wine must be grown and made in the relatively small, chilly region of the same name, Champagne, not too far from Paris. The majority of French sparkling wine made outside of Champagne is called crémant.*

Grapes

Champagne is primarily produced from three main grapes: Chardonnay, Pinot Noir and Pinot Meunier. They are thought to bring purity, weight and fruitiness to a blend, respectively. The four other grapes that are legally allowed but rarely seen are Pinot Blanc, Pinot Gris, Petit Meslier and Arbanne.

Processing the fruit

Champagne grapes are harvested earlier in their ripening cycle than is customary for still wine. This translates to higher levels of acidity and lower levels of alcohol, which is part of the reason the wines tend to be so bracing.

The elegance and transparency of champagne necessitates gentle handling of the fruit, which is pressed slowly and at low pressure. Unless the winery is producing a rosé, the skins are discarded straight away. As mentioned above, Champagne is one of the few places where rosé is created through the addition of a small amount of still red wine. And while that is permitted, it is not the only way to produce rosé champagne. Some wineries prefer to extract colour via a brief period of skin contact.

Primary fermentation

Most sparkling wines experience two fermentations: one that makes alcohol and one that makes bubbles. In Champagne, the result of the initial fermentation is referred to as *vin clair* and is effectively an austere white wine. Producers create, blend and age their *vins clairs* to achieve the desired flavour profile before subjecting the wines to the second fermentation.

Stainless steel is the most common fermentation vessel in Champagne, but some producers use barrels to impart a sense of richness or depth. Whether or not to allow malolactic fermentation (MLF) is another stylistic differentiator. Those that block MLF are seeking a brighter, livelier wine. Those that allow it are coaxing creaminess. MLF can also vary according to vintage, with producers preventing it in warmer years and encouraging it in cooler seasons.

Secondary fermentation

Once the *vins clairs* are blended, the wine is placed inside the same bottles you will ultimately enjoy it from several years hence. A small amount of yeast and sugar is added to the bottle, which is then sealed with a metal cap. The yeast consumes the sugar, which creates a small amount of alcohol and carbon dioxide (CO_2), aka bubbles!

Ageing

Champagne is kept in bottle for many months following its second fermentation. During this time, the yeast cells (lees) die and begin to slowly decompose. This unsavoury-sounding practice is called autolysis, and it releases all sorts of yummy stuff into the wine, including those tantalizing bakery aromas that so often mark great champagne.

To call itself champagne, a wine must age on its lees for a minimum of 15 months for a non-vintage style, and a minimum of 36 months for vintage-dated wines. Some luxury cuvées like Dom Pérignon age on their lees for seven to 10 years – occasionally longer. That's a very long time to perfect a wine and part of the reason why top-shelf champagnes can be so expensive.

During the ageing process, the bottles are incrementally adjusted so that the lees slowly collect in the neck. This process is called *riddling* and was historically conducted by hand, though today it is more commonly mechanized.

The next series of steps happen fast. To remove the yeast, the now-inverted bottle is frozen at its tip. Either man or machine pops off the cap, the frozen yeast plug shoots out, and a natural cork is inserted, along with handy cage. This separation of champagne from lees is known as disgorgement, and it is becoming common to see the disgorgement date listed on the label.

Above Riddling by hand is a laborious and historic practice.
Above right Machine-riddling is becoming increasingly common.

Dosage

When a bottle is disgorged, a small amount of wine is lost. A producer will typically compensate for this loss by adding a mixture of wine and sugar known as *dosage*. As discussed on page 29, sweetness was historically important to balance champagne's strident acidity. But while most producers still add some degree of *dosage*, this practice has decreased over time. This change is due both to consumer preferences trending dry and to climate change, which has increased overall ripeness levels. Riper fruit means lower natural acidity, therefore less of a need to soften the wine with sugar.

THE PROSECCO METHOD

Compared to the elaborate traditional method, the Prosecco approach is relatively simple. More commonly known as the Charmat method, this technique also involves two fermentations, but the second one occurs in a pressurized tank rather than in millions of individual bottles. This process is both faster and more efficient, and the wines can be bottled shortly after harvest.

- Prosecco is also made with different grapes to champagne, most notably the fruity and floral Glera variety.
- Because the Charmat method does not involve long ageing on the lees, the resulting wines rarely boast champagne's bread-like aroma.
- The Charmat method can be considered the better system for creating Prosecco, Moscato and Lambrusco, as the yeasty aromas imparted by the traditional method might interfere with their perfume.
- Prosecco doesn't enjoy the same high reputation as champagne, but the region is undergoing a massive revolution in quality. Higher-end Proseccos are well-worth seeking out and remain a bargain in comparison to most champagnes.

OTHER SPARKLERS

California sparkling wine

California is a massive place with few regulations in place to impede creativity. As a result, one can find a staggering array of sparkling styles. Still, the state is best known for its traditional method wines that rely on the mainstay champagne grapes of

Pinot Noir and Chardonnay. Many of California's best brands are outposts of the big Champagne houses themselves.

Cava

Made via the traditional method but using indigenous Spanish grapes (and sometimes Chardonnay), Cava remains one of the best value sparkling wines.

Crémant

A broad category of traditional method sparkling wine from France (that doesn't include Champagne). Most regional Crémant (Crémant de la Loire, Crémant d'Alsace, etc) requires a minimum ageing period of nine months on the lees, but the grape varieties used span the gamut.

English sparkling wine

The chalky soils of southeast England have proved a terrific place for sparkling wine. These often-austere beauties are mostly made in the image of champagne – Chardonnay and Pinot Noir crafted using the traditional method.

Franciacorta

Franciacorta is Italy's answer to champagne. It is made predominately from Pinot Noir (Pinot Nero in Italian) and Chardonnay, though smaller amounts of Pinot Blanc (Pinot Bianco) and Erbamat are allowed. The best wines are produced in tiny quantities and are often priced in line with champagne.

Lambrusco

Lambrusco is a complicated, misunderstood and occasionally thrilling category of wine. Still damaged by the ubiquity of Riunite in the 1970s and '80s ('On ice… that's nice!'), this product of Emilia-Romagna has been enjoying a quiet comeback among wine geeks

DECODING CHAMPAGNE LABELS

European wine labels are notoriously hard to read, and champagne has the added complication of its own dedicated lexicon. The following is a guide to some key terms:

Non-vintage (NV) A 'non-vintage' champagne is one made from a combination of many vintages. Because Champagne's climate is so marginal for wine growing, there were historically massive stylistic swings between years. Blending multiple vintages together therefore became the best way to create a consistently appealing product. Non-vintage (NV) is the most commonly seen term, but some producers and restaurants are switching to the technically more accurate 'multi-vintage (MV)'.

Grower-producer (RM) As a region, Champagne has an unusual structure, with hundreds of growers selling their fruit (or wine) to a handful of big 'houses', sometimes known as Grandes Marques. The past few decades have witnessed a shift, with an increasing number of growers becoming vertically integrated, producing and marketing their own wine. These so-called 'grower-producers' have been rising in prominence despite the artisan scale of their production. Their wine labels will be marked with a small RM (Récoltant-Manipulant), while the larger houses that don't grow all their own fruit will sport an NM (Négociant-Manipulant).

for a while now. It can be made in a variety of styles (red or rosé, sweet or dry) and either via Charmat or *méthode ancestrale*. The best examples are dry-ish and earthy with abundant dark fruit, but the category is still replete with fizzy pink frivolity.

Méthode Cap Classique

Méthode Cap Classique is a traditional method South African sparkling wine that must legally rest for a minimum of 12 months on its lees and can be made from any grape variety.

Blanc de Noirs This technically translates to 'white from red', meaning a white sparkling wine made from red grapes, either Pinot Noir, Pinot Meunier, or both.

Blanc de Blancs 'White from white.' Seeing *Blanc de Blancs* on a label usually implies that a champagne has been produced exclusively from Chardonnay, though technically Pinot Blanc and others are allowed.

Sweetness levels As previously stated, most champagnes include some degree of residual sugar. The level is always indicated on the label, via the terminology below. Note that there is overlap between many categories. This allows a producer to select the wording that best suits their brand identity and marketing.

Brut Nature	(also known as non-*dosé* and ultra brut): 0–3 grams per litre (g/l)
Extra Brut	0–6g/l
Brut	0–12g/l
Extra Dry	12–17g/l
Sec	17–32 g/l
Demi-Sec	32–50 g/l
Doux	50+ g/l

Pét-nat

Pét-nat's full name is '*pétillant-naturel*'; it is a sparkling wine made by an ancient technique called *méthode ancestrale*. This method differs from the traditional and Charmat process in that it involves only one fermentation, with the bubbles created on the first go-round. *Pét-nat* is either fermented entirely in bottle or is bottled halfway through fermentation, trapping the CO_2 in solution. The resulting wine is usually less sparkly than champagne and might even be cloudy if the producer elects not to disgorge. As the name implies, *méthode ancestrale* pre-dates champagne yet it has become quite modish, mostly due to the natural wine scene's interest in *pét-nat*.

Sekt

Sekt is a generic term for German sparkling wine, and the quality and style range widely. Most is produced by the Charmat method and results in cheap, cheerful and sometimes sweet bubbles. The best – which are truly very good – are Riesling-based dry wines made using the traditional method (though high-quality examples from Chardonnay and Pinot Noir are on the rise).

DESSERT WINE

Dessert wine is our most ancient style of wine. Prior to the advent of refrigeration, if you wanted a wine to last a really long time, the best strategy was for it to be sweet. Think of it like making jam, which is still the preferred way to extend the shelf life of fresh fruit.

A long-living wine was always a good thing but became especially important once man began making lengthy journeys across the sea. And though today we rarely transport casks of wines on ships, dessert wines still offer some practical advantages. Being naturally sturdy, sweet wines last a considerable time once opened; unfortified styles will stay fresh in your fridge for weeks while fortified examples may survive for months.

Unfortunately, dessert wine evolved from being an act of preservation to being in need of preservation. Global sales of sweet wines have been plummeting for a while now, especially at the premium end of the spectrum. Changes in consumer taste, attitudes towards health as pertains to alcohol consumption, and tightening drunk driving laws have all contributed to the decline. This is a shame on many levels, especially when you consider the category's rich variety of styles.

Dessert wines are made in all corners of the world and range from wispy and ethereal to syrupy sweet. The methods of manufacture span a similarly wide spectrum, as do the alcoholic potencies. But flavour offers the biggest bounty. From the profundity of port, the honeyed depths of Tokaji Aszú, the purity of Eiswein, the caramel perfume of Vin Santo, and the briny mysteries of old Madeira, dessert styles are truly unmatched in the world of wine.

STYLES AND PRODUCTION

There are many different ways to make dessert wine, but the end goal is the same: to leave unfermented sugar in the bottle. How this is achieved varies according to culture and location, but there are some common methodologies. Below are some of the dominant approaches and their most prominent examples.

It's worth pointing out that the processes employed to concentrate a grape's sugar often concentrate its other qualities as well at the same time, especially acidity and flavour. This is part of the magic of dessert wine. They are not just super-sweet versions of table wines, they are super-charged in all dimensions, bursting with lift and life.

DRIED GRAPES

Perhaps the most straightforward of dessert wines, the dried-fruit styles are created through the fermentation of raisins. These are made either by leaving the fruit on the vine for an extended time (weather permitting), or by drying it on mats in the sun or inside designated chambers.

The raisins are high in sugar, but they are also very low in moisture – imagine squeezing a raison versus a grape. Because of the smaller amount of liquid, it takes considerably more fruit to end up with a comparable volume of dessert wine. This is part of the reason why many sweet wines are more expensive than their dry counterparts.

We've already established that yeasts consume sugar and create alcohol but haven't yet covered that they will start to struggle once a certain alcohol level is achieved, which is generally around 15.5%. Table wines (aka, non-dessert styles) are harvested below that threshold, so the yeast can finish its job relatively easily. But raisins are so sweet that the yeast expires well before all the sugar is consumed, resulting in a naturally sweet wine.

That said, not all dried grape wines are the same. The precise details of fermentation and *élevage* vary widely. Some are fermented using solely raisins while others add only a small percentage of dried grapes into the mix. Some are aged in oak while others are bottled rapidly. The permitted grape varieties also range. The curious consumer will have to follow their own rabbit holes as options abound.

Famous examples:

Italy	Various passito and recioto styles, most notably Passito di Pantelleria and Recioto di Valpolicella; Vin Santo
France	Jurançon, Vendage Tardive, Vin de Paille, Vouvray Moelleux
Greece	Commandaria (Cyprus), Vinsanto
Elsewhere	Constantia (South Africa), late harvest (New World), straw wine (Australia, United States), Strohwein (Germany)

ICE WINE

Drying grapes is not the only way to concentrate sugars; there are less conventional methods as well. In the instance of ice wine, which is most commonly made in cold climate regions such as Germany's Mosel and Canada's Niagara, harvesting the grapes during a hard winter freeze does the trick. Because the water inside the grape freezes but the pulp does not, pressing extrudes the ice, leaving behind a concentrated nectar. The resulting wines are so profoundly sweet that they require a high level of acidity for balance. This is why exceptionally bracing varieties such as Riesling or the hybrid Vidal Blanc tend to be used in the production of ice wine.

Famous examples:

Germany and Austria	Eiswein
Canada and Northern United States	Icewine and ice wine, respectively

NOBLE ROT

For many grape growers, their worst enemies in the vineyard are mould, rot and mildew. And yet, in select parts of the world, a particular type of fungus makes for an interesting dessert wine. Known as botrytis (*Botrytis cinerea*), or noble rot, it penetrates the skin of the grape and sucks out the moisture, desiccating the fruit and concentrating its sugar, acidity and flavours.

The best botrytis wines are picked berry by berry, based on the depth of infection. This is enormously labour-intensive, which is often reflected in the price tag. Indeed, botrytis dessert wines are among the most expensive in the world, with Sauternes even being aged in pricey new French oak barrels – a rarity among dessert wines. These wines tend to be both rich and electric, with the added complexity of saffron, ginger or chamomile notes from the botrytis.

Top Grapes featuring varying degrees of botrytis (noble rot) infection.
Above A glass of honey-hued sweet Sauternes.

Famous examples:

Austria	Ausbruch, Trockenbeerenauslese (TBA)
France	Barsac, Bonnezeaux, Quarts de Chaume, Sauternes, Sélection de Grains Nobles (SGN)
Germany	Beerenauslese (BA), Trockenbeerenauslese (TBA)
Hungary	Tokaji Aszú

FORTIFIED WINES

Fortified wine is a specific subset of dessert wine wherein sweetness is achieved by adding a high proof spirit. Remember when I said yeast can only survive up to a certain alcohol level? Well, the sudden addition of neutral grape spirit will stop fermentation by shocking and killing the yeast, leaving behind uneaten sugar. This is roughly the way in which port and other fortified dessert wines are made.

Fortified is an historic style of winemaking that is closely associated with ocean voyages. Boosting the alcohol level of a wine not only created a sweet and tasty beverage, it also increased its durability.

Port is the most famous fortified wine, and an established model that has been iterated around the world. Ripe red grapes are harvested, crushed and allowed to begin fermentation. After a couple of days, once around a third of the sugar has been consumed, neutral grape spirit is added, which kills the yeast, resulting in a sweet, higher-proof style of red wine. From there, handling depends on the type of port being produced. Ruby ports (including vintage styles) are aged in bottle, while tawny ports are aged in cask to encourage oxidation.

Sherry is another well-known example, but here the spirit addition typically happens post-fermentation when the wine is dry. If sweetness is desired, it is normally added after the fact. An exception to this is Pedro Ximénez (PX), a somewhat obscure but delicious sherry made from dried grapes of the same name. The fermenting wine is fortified partway through fermentation, leaving behind a significant amount of sugar.

Madeira is unique among fortified styles. Not only was it able to withstand long ocean journeys, but the wine's taste was believed to benefit from the experience. The rough treatment it surely experienced on a ship, with prolonged exposure to the elements, is now approximated within the winery where it is deliberately heated and oxidized. Styles run from lightly to very sweet, with the dessert styles being fortified early in the fermentation process, as with port.

Great Madeiras truly are a marvel; the heat and oxidation add a curious savoury tang that can be something of an acquired taste at first but quickly becomes addictive. Madeiras are also notoriously long-lived, putting even the most stalwart dessert wine to shame. Lovers of sweet wine will want to seek out the more luscious styles of Malvasia and Boal/Bual.

Famous examples:

Portugal	Port, Madeira
Spain	Moscatel, Sherry
Elsewhere	Angelica (California), Marsala (Italy), Rutherglen Muscat (Australia), Samos (Greece), Vin Doux Naturel (France)

Note *The above is only a fraction of the whole. There are countless other dessert wines that don't fit neatly into these categories including Lambrusco, Brachetto d'Acqui, Moscato d'Asti, Asti Spumante, sweet styles of champagne, and a host of delicately saccharine wines like Germany's Auslesen. If sweet wine is your thing, this is good news. Take this list and run to your local wine store; they're bound to have something great for you.*

"

Madeira is unique among fortified styles. Not only was it able to withstand long ocean journeys, but the wine's taste was believed to benefit from the experience.

NATURAL WINE

Depending on where you are at in your wine life, the idea of natural wine likely either excites you or makes you feel old. I fall into the latter camp, which is why I'm not going to spend too much time talking about it, lest I out myself as the uncool bystander that I am.

'Natural wine' is a relatively recent phenomenon that is often misunderstood, in part because it lacks a firm definition and encompasses philosophic, stylistic and technical aspects. While often questioned by more traditional wine drinkers, natural wine is especially popular among younger audiences and could easily be thanked for attracting a more diverse drinking demographic.

The natural wine movement promotes the idea of 'low-intervention winemaking'. This term does not solely belong to natural wine; many conscientious producers seek to manipulate their wines as little as possible. But in the natural wine context it tends to mean limited sulphur additions, no new oak, reliance on ambient yeast, limited fining or filtration, no acidity (pH) or alcohol adjustments and no additives. Taken to the extreme, this style of winemaking can open the door to flaws, and indeed many natural wines express higher levels of volatile acidity, Brettanomyces and oxidation than is typically embraced. That said, there are plenty of natural wines that would be considered technically flawless.

Though I sometimes struggle to enjoy the edgier examples, I admire the spirit of the natural wine movement. Its producers routinely look beyond the archetypal regions of Burgundy, Bordeaux and Champagne for inspiration, turning instead to places like Georgia or Friuli. There is also often an appreciation of ancient styles and techniques such as orange wine and *méthode ancestrale* sparkling wines, amphora, whole cluster inclusion and non-mainstream grape varieties, including hybrids. This has injected much-needed creativity into an industry that can easily be criticized for being inflexible and stodgy.

My musical mind understands natural wine best in the context of punk. Both movements contain a youth culture element, an anti-establishment feel and a hint of social revolution. They are also both empowering to 'outsiders'. It's important to mention that many young people or new drinkers can no longer afford access to the previous generation's reference point wines such as Grand Cru Burgundy or top Napa Cabernet. And so, the need to create a new suite of icons, heroes and traditions arose.

But despite the way the media talks about it, natural wine is not a religion. You do not have to be 'all in' to participate. Play around, explore and come up with your own conclusions. There are some seriously fun wines to discover.

Below Though small barrels hewn from French oak have become commonplace, there are a variety of wooden vessels available to winemakers.

ALL ABOUT BARRELS

Today, barrels are associated almost exclusively with wine and spirits. But for thousands of years, they were as mundane as cardboard boxes and just as universally employed. Barrels evolved shortly after the dawn of the Common Era as a more durable alternative to clay amphorae, the preferred carrying case of the Ancient Egyptians, Greeks and Romans.

The importance of barrels spiked during the Colonial Era, when they proved essential for shipping small goods and liquids – everything from wine to bullets to turnips – between Europe and the colonies. The barrel was prized for its round shape, which made it easy to roll, but its extreme weight when full meant that it couldn't be carried. Because of this, transportation occurred primarily over water, and only later via railway or automotive.

The aftermath of the Industrial Revolution witnessed the triple advents of cardboard, stainless steel and plastic. This revolutionized many industries, packing and shipping among them. Soon, the barrel was set aside, but the ever-sentimental wine and spirits industries held on a bit longer. At this point in time, most wines were still sold by the cask, with merchants handling the bottling directly. This practice persisted until sometime after World War II, when it became more common for wineries to bottle their production themselves.

It's not clear when the wine-barrel relationship shifted from friends to bedfellows, but these days it would be almost weird if a red wine wasn't aged in some sort of wooden vessel. Not only does a barrel's porosity help soothe and smooth a wine's tannins but the scent of the wood is prized by many for adding aromatic complexity.

Though certain parts of the world prefer chestnut or acacia, and redwood was used for tanks in early American wine history, oak is most commonly employed. Still, not all oak species make good candidates for barrels. Close your eyes and picture the twisting, moss-covered oaks of northern California and the Deep South. Now imagine trying to cut a straight plank from them; you'd waste half the tree! Only the most vertical oak tree species make sense, especially those grown in cool regions and on poor soils. Such conditions slow growth, which results in a tighter grain.

French oak dominates the international wine industry, especially at the higher end, with winemakers even noting the differences between forests. Hungarian and Austrian oak are gaining in

> **Not only does a barrel's porosity help soothe and smooth a wine's tannins but the scent of the wood is prized by many for adding aromatic complexity.**

popularity and American oak, once considered too garish for fine wine, is undergoing a qualitative revolution. But no matter the source, the process remains the same: planks are hewn and left out in the elements for up to five years. This essential step seasons the wood before it is bent into shape, either by steam or, more commonly, by fire.

All these elements – the species of oak, country and forest of origin, length of ageing, and means of bending, not to mention the thickness of the staves, the size of the barrel and the skill of the cooper – make for an almost limitless combination of attributes. It is not uncommon for a winery to work with a wide array of barrels and winemakers spend considerable energy matching forest to cuvée. They do this because the barrel has a shaping effect on the wine, sometimes subtle, sometimes overt, but never actually neutral.

Not too bad for a glorified cardboard box.

SULPHUR AND ITS MISCONCEPTIONS

There is no single subject within wine as poorly understood as sulphur. I am constantly fielding questions about it. Consumers blame sulphur for their headaches and some members of the wine trade villainize it as an element of industrial winemaking. Neither position is completely valid.

Below, I have outlined some of the common queries that come my way. Hopefully, the answers I've set out will help to dispel some of the more stubborn sulphur myths...

WHAT DOES SULPHUR DO AND WHY IS IT ADDED TO WINE?

Sulphur dioxide (SO2) has been used in winemaking for hundreds of years. It is a naturally occurring compound that is both anti-microbial and antioxidant. This means that a little SO2 not only keeps bad bacteria and yeast from spoiling your wine, but it also helps prevent oxidation. In fact, sulphur dioxide's extreme and multifaceted usefulness has led to widespread application across the greater food and beverage industries.

Note that sulphur comes in many forms. When it is being added to a food or drink, it is normally in the form of SO2, which is also known as sulphites. A different form of sulphur called 'elemental sulphur' is applied to vineyards to stave off mildew and other fungal diseases. Elemental sulphur can also be used to sanitize empty wine barrels.

WHY DOES WINE HAVE SO MANY SULPHITES?

It doesn't! At least, not compared to many other foodstuffs. The average glass of wine is about 10 parts per million (ppm) sulphites, which is about the same as in a handful of dried fruit. Sports drinks can contain two or three times that amount and pre-made salad dressing as much as nine times. Potato chips, canned soup, candy, shrimp and maple syrup also contain elevated levels of sulphites. Furthermore, because sulphites are naturally produced by yeast during fermentation, they sometimes appear in wines that had zero sulphites added.

Part of the reason so many consumers associate wine with high levels of sulphites is because several countries mandated that producers slap a 'contains sulphites' warning on their wine labels. Sulphur-defenders argue that this brought undue attention to the compound, especially as wineries aren't required to list any other additives.

WHICH WINES HAVE THE MOST SULPHITES?

Because tannins provide additional antioxidant support, red wines require fewer sulphites. Sweet wines, however, require extra as sugar binds to the sulphites, rendering them ineffective. Sparkling wines also contain more sulphites on average than still wine; prized for their freshness, a higher level of SO2 helps stave off any unwelcome oxidation.

Here is how the major wine categories rank, from lowest sulphites to highest:

- Dry red wines
- Dry white wines
- Champagne and sparkling wines
- Dessert wines

DO EUROPEAN WINES HAVE LESS SULPHUR?

On average, European wines have the same level of sulphur as American and other New World wines.

The main confusion stems from the fact that, legally, Europe has a lower ceiling on total allowed sulphites. The maximum sulphites a European producer can add is 160ppm for dry red wines and 210ppm for dry white wines. In the United States, the upper legal limit is 350ppm for all wines, but in practice European and American wineries tend to use around the same. The average level of sulphites found in a dry red wine, irrespective of country of origin, is around 80ppm.

DOES ORGANIC WINE HAVE LESS SULPHUR?

This is confusing, but (at least according to the United States government) there is a big difference between 'organic wine' and 'wine made from organic grapes' – a distinction that is advertised on the label. In the US, organic wine can't have any added sulphites, but up to 40ppm may occur naturally during fermentation. Wine made from organic grapes, however, can have up to 100ppm.

That figure of 100ppm is more than the dry red wine average. So, unless you are buying an 'organic wine' (which is a far rarer category than 'wine made from organic grapes') there may not be a measurable difference in sulphites between it and a non-organically farmed option.

If low or no sulphites are important to you, I suggest looking into natural wines. 'Sans souffre', which means 'without sulphur', is a popular category within that genre.

WHY DOES SULPHUR GIVE ME A HEADACHE?

If drinking wine gives you a headache, it's probably not the sulphites. That's not to say you're not sensitive to them – many are, especially asthmatics, and should limit their exposure accordingly. But statistically very few people are actually *allergic* to sulphur.[1]

And besides, if sulphites were the culprit, you would also experience discomfort every time you ate French fries or heated up a can of soup. If that's not the case, there's a good chance the fault lies elsewhere.

What, then, is causing all these wine headaches?

Dehydration and over-indulgence are very real considerations, and certainly can lead to headaches. But, historically, if someone complained specifically of a *red wine headache* (red wine being lower in sulphites than white wine), the blame was placed on tannins, histamines or biogenic amines, all of which are present in greater amounts in red wines.

That 'diagnosis' gained traction in the industry, but the data to support it was thin. Which is why the new research coming out of University of California, Davis, is so exciting. A compound named quercetin has been identified as the potential culprit. In grapes, it is located in the skins, which would explain why it is associated

---

[1] Note: I am a wine geek, not a doctor. If drinking wine gives you headaches, please consult a medical professional.

more closely with red wine than white. Quercetin effectively blocks the body's natural digestion of alcohol, resulting in an increase of the inflammatory compound acetaldehyde in the bloodstream. This can cause headaches and, occasionally, nausea.

Though human trials have yet to be conducted, the research looks very promising. Hopefully a deeper understanding of this mechanism will provide relief for many and remove some of the stigma from sulphur.

WHY DON'T SOME WINE PROFESSIONALS LIKE SULPHUR?

Some wine professionals, especially those that identify with the natural wine movement, criticize what they see as the industry's over-reliance on sulphur. Sulphur can be applied at many stages in a wine's life, but it is most commonly added just after picking and right before bottling. The former addition knocks back any ambient or spoilage yeast, helping ensure that Saccharomyces (which is fairly sulphur-resistant) will dominate the fermentation, whether inoculated or not. The latter addition ensures that the wine is shelf-stable, and hopefully prolongs its life.

Why would these things be considered bad?

Well, some believe that restricting a fermentation to Saccharomyces reduces complexity in a wine, and that interfering with ambient yeast populations obfuscates site expression (aka terroir). As to the shelf-stability question, that's a bit more complicated. For while sulphur giveth in terms of fortitude and longevity, it also taketh away – if abused, too much sulphur can mute flavours and warp texture.

I am personally in favour of a judicious use of sulphur. More than once I've ordered a low or no sulphur wine in a restaurant only to be served a diminished version of what should have been spectacular. But I've also suffered through more than one bottle that had its character snuffed out due to aggressive sulphur usage. As with so many things in wine, moderation is key.

CORKS, BOTTLES AND ALTERNATIVES

Like many wine drinkers, I have a love/hate relationship with corks. I love the ceremonies surrounding their extrusion, collect my favourites as souvenirs, and even enjoy wrestling with a difficult one. Nearly all the great wines of my life have been bottled under cork.

But the heartbreak of cork taint is not easily healed. Accounts vary, but for most of my career, the accepted wisdom was that five percent of all corks were infected with TCA (*see* pages 42–43). That's at least one bottle in every two cases! The wine industry lived with this vile statistic for a very long time – it simply didn't have a choice. That is, until alternative closures began to gain traction.

Screw caps were and remain the most prominent substitution, with Australia their most fervent proponent. I remember when they were first getting popular in the US. People regarded them with high suspicion and sommeliers were stymied by their pop-and-pour vibe. Eventually, consumer comfort increased, but only for white wines or inexpensive reds. Age-worthy reds, most agreed, required natural cork to evolve

Being a natural product that can be harvested without harming its tree, corks actually boast a negative carbon footprint.

in the cellar. Recently, however, the screw cap industry introduced technology that allows a small amount of oxygen to permeate the closure, the idea being that this will allow wines to age gracefully over extended periods.

Meanwhile, the cork industry underwent its own technological revolution. It has done an admirable job of minimizing cork taint in recent years. If so desired, a producer can select corks that are pre-screened for TCA, which virtually eliminates the risk. Some corks are even scanned for cellular uniformity, as invisible defects in the interior of the cork might lead to oxidation down the road. The cork companies have also doubled down on their positive attributes, especially as pertains to environmental health and waste management. Being a natural product that can be harvested without harming their tree, corks actually boast a negative carbon footprint, which helps offset the emissions released in the production of glass.

Many corks are punched whole out of the thick bark of a mature cork oak tree.

Speaking of glass, bottles are also under scrutiny, with alternative packaging on the rise. Cans are increasingly popular, especially poolside, at concerts or at sporting events – basically anywhere a corkscrew and glass wouldn't be appropriate. Bag-in-box is another fast-growing trend, though it was always popular in Scandinavia. Like cans, bag-in-box is touted for its increased sustainability and lower carbon footprint.

As with screw caps before them, these alternative containers were initially reserved for lower-tier wines. But as the marketplace gets comfortable with this change, higher quality wine is making the jump.

Having said all that, as someone who likes to buy wine to age, I'll likely stick to bottles and corks for most of my purchases. But a can of wine after a long hike is a beautiful thing. Especially if you're like me, and constantly misplacing your corkscrew.

8

Growing Wine

When I first started in the wine industry, I thought winemakers were gods. I attended as many tastings as I could and hung on their every word, certain that the secrets to wine's greatness lay in some special insight or twist of the wrist. And when I finally started travelling to the various wine regions of the world, I eagerly shuffled between cellar, fermentation hall and tasting room. The only soil I saw was in jars.

Beyond their location on a map, I hardly ever thought about vineyards. And farming never crossed my mind. Twenty-plus years later, I am consumed by viticulture.

It is a common trope in the wine industry that 'great wine is made in the vineyard'. Needless to say, this is not literally true; we know that multiple people – and not just the winemaker – are responsible for the success of any given wine. But what is quite literally true is that the vineyard sets the upper limit of a wine's quality. Even the most talented winemaker is not an alchemist. They cannot forge greatness from mediocrity.

If a winemaker needed to shin up a tree every time they wanted some grapes, there would be a whole lot less wine in the world. "

Site selection is paramount. The soil composition of a given place combined with its elevation, slope, microclimate and access to water determines much of the character of a wine. But farming is just as important. A great site could be pummelled to death by careless management. Perfect exposition and drainage hardly matter if the life is stripped from the soils through an overuse of herbicides, or if the vines are mercilessly overcropped or disease has been left to run rampant.

Looking out over a well-tended vineyard, it's easy to see only green tranquility. To view the rows of trunks and leaves as just another natural wonder, as self-organizing as a forest. But even the most placid vineyard is the result of hundreds of decisions that, in many ways, are the real sum of a wine's potential.

AN OVERVIEW OF VITICULTURE

As discussed on page 157, the majority of vines used for winemaking come from a single species: *Vitis vinifera*. It might seem a bit restrictive to limit the scope of wine to a single species but rest assured, there are over 10,000 different grape varieties within that species, nearly 1,500 of which are in commercial use! And all those vines have something in common: they do not want to behave in the way you see in vineyards.

Vines are climbers. Given its druthers, a grape vine would crawl along the ground until it found a tree to ascend. And once it broke through the canopy into the sunlight, it would throw out some leaves and a few clusters of grapes. The way vines are trained for wine production is completely unnatural, yet the alternative is impractical. If a winemaker needed to shin up a tree every time they wanted some grapes, there would be a whole lot less wine in the world.

And so, we bend and prune and twist and braid our vines into more manageable shapes. And the particular form they take is a key component of viticulture. But before we can understand how trellising and farming can influence a wine, we must first examine the vine itself.

A great site can take many forms:
Opposite top A terraced vineyard in Sonoma County, California.
Opposite middle The red clay vineyards of Rioja in northeast Spain.
Opposite bottom The beautiful vineyards of Riquewihr (Alsace) nestle in the shelter of the Vosges Mountains.

ANATOMY OF A VINE

No matter what shape they take, all vines contain the same basic parts. From the bottom to the top, these are: roots, trunk, branches, shoots, leaves and fruit.

Roots

Most vines are grafted onto American rootstocks. This practice began as a way to ward off phylloxera but has since evolved considerably. Now, rootstocks are engineered not only for their pest resistance but also for site compatibility. A farmer can select a rootstock based on its ability to withstand drought, endure wet conditions, thrive at either high or low soil pH/acidity, tolerate high salt content or nutritional deficiencies, suppress disease or generate high yields.

Roots can extend down several metres, with the precise depth depending on soil structure, vine age and farming style. If heavily irrigated, the roots will hover closer to the surface of the soil; if dry-farmed, they will extend deeper down in search of moisture. This can be beneficial because the further the roots dig, the greater array of materials they will encounter. And vines need to feast on a host of micronutrients to survive, specifically nitrogen, phosphorous, potassium, magnesium, boron, zinc, manganese, iron and copper.

Fun fact: roots aren't actually capable of absorbing these minerals themselves. They require fungi and bacteria to break them down. Science has recently discovered a barter system; we now know that the vines feed the surrounding fungal networks sugar in exchange for digestible forms of micronutrients. This realization has shed new light on the importance of soil health and the role of microbes.

Trunk

The trunk is the permanent wood that connects a vine's roots to its branches. Trunks gain thickness with age and function as the storage site for much of a vine's nutritional reserves, such as carbohydrates. The height of the trunk is set by the farmer according to the an area's climate, the vine's trellising system and local customs. For example, in Bordeaux, where it tends to be colder, the trunks are very short, so the clusters are closer to the ground and can absorb radiant heat from the soil. While in Rías Baixas (Spain) the trunks are often taller than a person so that the ground beneath and between them can be cultivated with other crops.

Branches

In viticulture, a vine's 'branches' are known as either canes or cordons. Both are woody protrusions from the trunk from which fruit-bearing shoots derive. In cane-pruning, the wood is always thin and flexible, as a new cane is formed every year. In cordon (or spur) pruning, a permanent branch is allowed to form, and so the wood becomes hard and thickens with age. Cordons and canes are arranged to form a vine's 'trellis', and there are dozens of different trellising systems employed all over the world. A vine's trellising system has a major impact, affecting everything from yield to the speed of ripening to the fruit's ability to withstand various weather events. For example, the shade of a head-trained vine protects its fruit from sunburn in hot climates.

In modern viticulture, cordons and canes are trained along wires; this creates the stripy patterns in vineyards so familiar to wine lovers. It also allows for a uniform fruit zone, the easy use of tractors and facilitates mechanical harvesting. Old vine vineyards,

Below left An example of cordon pruning, wherein permanent branches are allowed to form.

Below right Cane pruning, where flexible new branches are allowed to form each year.

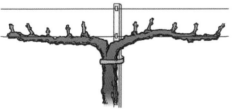

Cordon pruning **Cane pruning**

which tend to be head-trained, rarely feature wires; nor do the steeply inclined vineyards of the Mosel and Northern Rhône, where the vines are tied to stakes.

Shoots

Shoots are baby branches that form off a cane or cordon; they are a vital part of the vine that produces both leaves and fruit. Shoots emerge from buds, and only the best-positioned buds are allowed to grow. Ideally, the shoots will be at least a hand-width apart, which offers the benefit of well-spaced fruit (crowded or touching grape clusters could invite mould). In high-quality farming, it is customary to see one to three clusters of grapes per shoot.

Leaves

Leaves are the engine of the vine and therefore are of primary importance. Not only do they contain the chlorophyll that drives photosynthesis and creates fuel for the vine, but their pores assist in the exchange of vital gases. The shape created by the leaves at the top of the vine is known as the 'canopy', and this provides critical shelter, protecting fruit from direct exposure to the sun – grapes sunburn easier than British tourists! Having said that, too many leaves can impede ripening, so the perfect balance must be struck.

Fruit

It is important to remember that the grapevine is not interested in making wine; the grapevine only wants to make grapes. Grapes, or more specifically the seeds they carry, represent a vine's children, and, just like human beings, much of a vine's behaviour is guided by its desire to perpetuate its own species. This is the whole reason that grapes get sweet as soon as their seeds are hard enough to survive the digestive tract of an animal! The vine doesn't care about potential alcohol or tannin resolution – it wants an animal to eat its fruit and pass out the seed somewhere favourable. Ideally, far away from any winemakers.

MAKING BABY VINES

Despite the intentions of the plant, commercial grapevines are not propagated via seeds. They are reproduced asexually through cuttings. In this way, vintners can ensure genetic uniformity in their vineyard.

In other words, if you plant a Grenache cutting, you know that the resulting plant will also look and taste like Grenache. But if you plant a seed taken from a Grenache grape, there's no real way to know what the results might be. Anytime a genetic recombination is involved, things get unpredictable. My sister and I have the same two parents, but we look and act completely differently. We may share certain traits, such as an inability to look good in hats, but only one of us can retile a roof and it isn't me.

The omega cut, pictured above, is commonly employed by nurseries when bench-grafting young vine cuttings onto protective roots.

Genetic recombination isn't always a bad thing; it is the way in which all our current varieties evolved. For example, Cabernet Sauvignon is the result of a wild and long-ago crossing of Sauvignon Blanc and Cabernet Franc. But for every happy hypoallergenic Labradoodle there are hundreds of sterile stubborn mules. Randall Grahm, the legendary California winemaker turned grape-breeder, would agree. He is actively trying to create new varieties at his California property, Popelouchum, that will hopefuly be uniquely suited to their environment.

Grapes sunburn easier than British tourists!

ESTABLISHING A VINEYARD

Viticulture is unique within agriculture in that the vines stay in place for between 25 and 100 (plus!) years. Even if a winery turns over its vineyards rapidly, any decision lasts at least a generation. Because of this, every step of the development process needs to be rigorously examined. And there are a host of variables to consider.

To develop a successful vineyard, two things need to happen. One, the details need to be customized to the specific conditions of the site. And two, the viticultural strategy needs to be reverse engineered from the intended style of wine.

What does that mean? Well, customizing details to site could include such scenarios as using a low-vigour rootstock on a particularly fertile area to balance vine growth. Or increasing the space between vines in a dry area to reduce competition for natural resources.

And reverse engineering the viticultural strategy from the intended style of wine basically means that the wine informs the farming. If the goal is to produce a lot of cheap wine, high-vigour rootstocks will be selected, and the vines will be trellised to maximize output. If, on the other hand, the aim is to craft a premium product, decisions will be made that restrict yield and emphasize slow and even ripening. For example, orienting the vine rows to follow the path of the sun will ensure that both sides of the vine get similar exposure to light and heat.

The following are the basic steps of establishing a vineyard:

Soil work

A vineyard manager will assess the soil – its composition, water-holding capacity, pH, nutritional availability, pest-pressure, etc. They may install drainage, remove rocks, treat with amendments such as compost or lime or decide to leave it fallow for a few years based on the results.

   Note *Leaving a vineyard fallow is an expensive decision but often a good one, as it tends to restore soil health and fertility. As an added benefit, if there are pests present that feed on vines, a fallow field will starve them out.*

Layout

The next step is to physically lay out the vineyard. It is customary for a larger site to be subdivided into blocks, which are often based on variations in soil or topography. Row direction needs to be set; this is most frequently determined by the physical dimensions of the plot, with long rows generally preferred to short rows so there are fewer turns for a tractor to take. At the highest end of the quality spectrum, the sun's pathway and wind patterns might also be brought into consideration vis-à-vis row direction. Vine density is another concern and tends to be informed by the availability of natural resources (water, nutrients, etc) and intended trellising style. For instance, if the vines are going to support huge canopies with lots of fruit, they need to be spaced further apart.

Planting vines

Planting the vines comes next, which is more complicated than it sounds. Rootstocks need to be selected – either one stock or a mix – based on the physical characteristics of the site. These can either be pre-grafted to the intended grape variety in a nursery or grafted in the field. Field grafting involves allowing a rootstock to grow on its own for one or more years, then grafting it in the vineyard once the stock is sturdy enough. This is labour intensive but has the benefit of ensuring a strong root system, which is especially helpful if the intent is to dry-farm (not irrigate).

   The types of wine grapes are also selected around this time, though producers often know what they want to grow before even breaking the ground. As previously discussed, most varieties come in a range of clones, which is another decision to ponder. The vineyard manager then needs to determine where each variety will go. Microclimate often plays a role – I know of a mountaintop vineyard where the grower put Cabernet Sauvignon on the warmer south-facing slope and Riesling on the cooler north-facing slope, thereby tapping into each variety's climatic preferences.

Training vines

Once the vine is planted, it must be trained; otherwise, it will simply snake along the ground until it finds something fun to climb. Trellising systems vary widely. Some regions form their vines into bushes, which provide great shade but make harvest a bit of a scavenger hunt. Other places train their vines onto high pergolas, with the fruit dangling just overhead. But for much of modern viticulture, the standard practice is to use a stake to encourage the development of a vertical trunk, and then to manipulate the vine's branches (canes, cordons) along wires, forming rows. The height of the trunk, length and number of branches, and shape of the leafy canopy are all further considerations, each with their own pros and cons.

Once the vine is planted, it must be trained; otherwise it will simply snake along the ground until it finds something fun to climb.

CLONES

We've established that new vines are grown when cuttings are taken from existing vines, then are grafted and planted. In this way, the baby and the mother vine are genetically identical. In the world of science fiction, this would be considered a 'clone', but that is not what the wine industry means when it uses that term.

Over the course of many years, even if all the vines in a vineyard came from the same source, differences begin to emerge. A vineyard manager might notice that one vine is particularly vigorous, or that another's clusters form a slightly different shape. These subtle evolutions are the result of point mutations – natural occurrences that can arise through environmental triggers, viral infection, or simply during routine cellular division (aka, growth).

If the change is positive, that vine can be flagged, propagated and sold as a specific 'clone' of the given variety. Historically, this was a matter of natural selection; vineyard owners simply selected their strongest vines for cuttings. But today, you can shop for clones in a catalogue according to their specific attributes.

For example, in California, Clone 4 Chardonnay is known for its consistency and productivity, but some grumble its wines can be a bit dull. Whereas the Old Wente clone is praised for setting smaller berries, which concentrate flavour and make for a more characterful wine.

DO VINES NEED TO SUFFER TO MAKE GREAT WINE?

Way back in the pre-monoculture days when most farms were mixed-use, people would sow their fruits and vegetables in their best land and relegate their grapevines to their rockiest, least fertile pockets. Why? Because grape vines are plucky little plants that can basically grow anywhere. The magical accident of fate was that this resulted in better wine. It all comes down to focusing a vine's attention.

If you plant a vine in pure potting soil and provide unlimited water, it will grow and grow and throw a ton of leaves and maybe eventually get around to producing a cluster or two. Grow that same vine in a pile of rocks and it's going to result in a much smaller plant, with far fewer leaves, and – hopefully – tastier fruit. The vine's diminutive size will be partly a result of the lack of nutrition and water provided by our imaginary rockpile; but it will also be due to the vine's decision to focus its energy – it's literal carbohydrates and micronutrients – on ripening its fruit.

Remember – the grape seeds are the vine's children. If a vine doesn't feel as if it has enough to eat, it's at the very least going to make sure its kids are fed. After all, that's the best way to ensure the survival of its bloodline. Grapevines, they're just like us!

A word about old vines

There is a magic quality to old vines and their wines. That same wonder I feel when walking through ancient ruins comes upon me in certain historic vineyards. But old vines are almost more remarkable than Roman columns in that they are still alive! And they continue to produce delicious wines year after year.

Vines are funny creatures. It takes several years for them to put forth a meaningful crop. Consensus is lacking but many producers say the fruit only starts tasting 'mature' once the vines hit 15 years old. Then there's a golden period of about 20 years before overall production starts to decline. This is part of the reason why so many growers replant their vineyards every 35 years or so. After that age, they start to decline due to individual vine death.

Defenders of old vines would counter that what such vineyards lack in productivity, they make up for in quality. And I'll admit that I often find a deeper level of complexity in old vine wines. Old vines are also more resilient. They have a remarkable ability to conserve resources when under duress and to survive extreme conditions. The thinking is that an old vine has already lived through drought, flood, intense heat and frost, and therefore has the 'wisdom' to navigate those hardships. That may sound mystical, but anecdotal evidence supports the claim. In the recent California drought (2012–16), it was the younger, less established vines that died first, though other factors such as poor rootstocks may have contributed.

A YEAR IN THE VINEYARD

Harvest happens once a year. Imagine that! A seasoned winemaker recently bragged about his 45th harvest. This means he's only done his job 45 times, which doesn't sound like a lot. Even gymnasts, who enjoy notoriously short careers, compete in more than 45 meets.

The rarity of harvests over a lifetime creates a certain pressure to get everything right. Thankfully, humans have been making wine for a long time so there's considerable collective wisdom to draw upon. Still, there's a lot of things that happen during the course of a year that influence the potential success of a harvest, and much can go wrong. Vigilance and attention to detail are essential.

Winter

Following harvest, a vine's leaves will turn colour, dry and fall off. This is called senescence, and it marks the beginning of a period of dormancy for the vine. During the winter months, the vine resembles a small barren tree. If cuttings are to be taken for future propagation, now is the time. Many farmers focus on building soil health in winter, either by ploughing, sowing seeds for cover crop or adding compost to the vine rows.

Spring

In early spring/late winter, vines are pruned back to allow new growth to form. Once the soil temperature is warm enough, a hormonal signal is activated that initiates a process known as 'budbreak'. This is a sensitive time – the little fuzzy buds are fragile and easily damaged by frost, wind or hail. But assuming they survive undisturbed, the buds slowly unfurl to reveal tiny shoots that grow rapidly upwards to create the trellis and canopy. Eventually, small groupings of flowers appear that will become this year's fruit. These flowers open in late spring, which is another tense moment in viticulture. Most of the grape vines used for wine are hermaphroditic, which means they can pollinate themselves. Even so, a strong wind or heavy rainfall is all it takes to interfere with the 'fruit set'.

Summer

Summer is a frenetic time. Growers must ensure the canopy maintains its shape, which often involves a fair amount of tucking and trimming. Cover crops either die naturally, are turned into the soil or are mowed to a manageable length. Slowly, the miniature green grapes swell and sweeten. A critical event called '*veraison*' happens roughly four to six weeks after flowering; during this period the berries start to change colour. Sometimes, if clusters are too slow to turn,

Pictured right *Though much of the attention is given to summer time and harvest, vineyard work is a year-round endeavour.*

they might be cut off, which allows the vine to focus its energy on the better-performing bunches.

Autumn/fall

No matter how thoroughly one prepares, autumn comes crashing like a timpani and the final few weeks before harvest are always manic. If they haven't started already, winemakers will begin measuring the amount of sugar in the grapes, which is the primary indication of ripeness. Later, when it's time to call a pick date, other metrics such as acidity or tannin might be studied.

In many parts of the world, autumn storms are a menace. The appearance of one on a radar can send crews scrambling to pick, though some producers may elect to wait things out. The risks are high. If a winery harvests early to avoid a rainstorm, they might make slightly underripe wine. If they wait until afterwards, they gamble with flavour dilution and mould. But in some glorious years and in certain special places, no dice need be rolled; the weather remains genial and the winemaker can pick at his leisure.

Cover crops: it's not just grass and grapes

Chances are, you haven't thought too much about cover crops. I don't blame you. To the untrained eye, they likely resemble little more than your neighbour's unkempt yard.

But the reality is that cover crops are a dynamic and increasingly important component of quality viticulture. Winemakers and grape growers spend considerable time each year deciding which mix to plant, and each has its own special attributes. For example, the wide root of a daikon radish helps to aerate soil and fight compaction; brassicas scare off vine-nibbling nematodes by emitting a repellent odour, and clover captures atmospheric nitrogen and releases it into the soil.

Cover crops also help prevent erosion, increase vine stress (a good thing) in particularly wet or fertile areas, sequester carbon, add nutrients to the soil, retain moisture, attract beneficial insects, cultivate a healthy microbiome and reduce soil temperatures. During a recent heat spike a winemaker confessed to me that he

INSIDE TRACK
MICROCLIMATE

Microclimate is all-important in wine. Two plots right next to each other might look exactly alike and share the same soils, but a subtle difference in microclimate can have a measurable impact on the final wine. These differences might include humidity, sun exposure, wind patterns and temperature, among other factors.

Microclimates do not exist solely in a wine context. Your neighbourhood, perhaps even your own yard, has microclimates. Do you garden? At my house we have six different garden beds. One lies right in the path of the wind as compared the surface temperature of two adjacent rows – one that had been recently ploughed and one that remained under cover crop. The bare soil was 66°C (150°F) while the grassy row was 24°C (75°F)!

The current raging debate is whether to plough the cover crops into the ground or to keep them growing year-round. Ploughing releases carbon into the atmosphere but is also the best way to get the nutrients from the cover crops into the soil where they can feed the vines. A third option is to 'crimp' the cover crop, which bends the plants into a kind of moist thatch just above the ground. While something of a niche practice, crimping has been gaining in popularity as concerns about carbon emissions have risen.

Cover crops also help increase vine stress (a good thing)... "

it curves around the house and also receives an extra hour of shade. It is therefore much cooler than the others and so is where we plant our lettuces. On the opposite side of the yard, a different bed enjoys unbroken sunshine and is far more protected from the wind. This is where we grow our peppers and tomatoes.

Our yard is not large, and yet there are significant enough variations in microclimate that our choice of planting site effects the performance of our produce. Wine grapes are arguably even more sensitive.

RETHINKING GRAPE VARIETIES

It can be frustrating. Just when you think you have a handle on a certain wine region, something changes. Perhaps a novel appellation is declared, some new regulation is introduced, or an important winery closes. These are dynamic times, and though wine is more mired in tradition than other comestible products, it still evolves. And when it comes to climate change – wine's most urgent crisis – much of the discussion seems to centre around rethinking which grape varieties should grow, and where.

Thankfully, the industry in general, but especially younger drinkers, is more and more open-minded on this point. The Finger Lakes in upstate New York makes a great case study. One of the most celebrated moments in its history is when Russian scientist Dr Konstantin Frank was able to successfully grow *Vitis vinifera* in the 1950s. This lone act is credited with sparking a fine wine revolution in the region. The thing is, the Finger Lakes had been making wine for a hundred years at that point. It just wasn't considered 'fine'.

The Finger Lakes boasts an incredibly marginal climate; winters get so cold that vines need to be buried to avoid debilitating frost damage. Because of this, vinifera's performance is irregular, and the life of its tenders can be stressful. Indigenous American grapes and vinifera-American hybrids are easier and cheaper to grow. Adapted to local conditions, these hearty vines put out reliable crops and, providing there is commercial interest in their output, offer greater financial stability to the growers. The market's increasing flexibility regarding non-vinifera wines has been a boon to this remote and frosty region.

Over in France, change comes slowly but it comes all the same. In 2019, Bordeaux announced it had approved the inclusion of seven new grape varieties, specifically selected as a response to climate change. As with its traditional roster of Cabernet Sauvignon, Merlot and Sauvignon Blanc, these vines are pure vinifera, but have proven to be successful in warmer climates, are more heat-resistant and better able to tolerate drought. Though they are only allowed at a maximum of 10 percent of a wine's final blend, this initiative, coming from one of Europe's most traditional and esteemed regions, startled the notoriously conservative wine industry.

Back in the time of Ancient Greece, wine was often blended or diluted prior to drinking. Pine sap, honey, spices, even saltwater were regularly utilized to adjust a wine's potency, prolong its life, or enhance its flavour. Aside from the lingering presence of Retsina, a speciality Greek wine steeped with resin, this practice had disappeared from the annals of fine wine. Except that *Decanter* magazine, arguably the industry's standard-bearer, recently published a column extolling the virtues of a wine made from the French-American hybrid Vidal Blanc co-fermented with honey. From Maryland, no less.

What does all this mean for the wine industry? Are blended or non-vinifera wines going to take over the marketplace? Will collectors set aside Oregon Pinot Noir for a glass of Scuppernong?

Of course not. A rising interest in more obscure grapes, places and practices poses no threat to the traditional wine landscape. In fact, I would argue that it's a purely positive phenomenon. A greater selection of wine flavours, price points and approaches equals more ways in for the budding wine enthusiast!

The world is changing, and new challenges are being revealed. Wine adapts and is much the better for it. An adaptable wine drinker is also sure to be rewarded.

Will collectors set aside Oregon Pinot Noir for a glass of Scuppernong?

INSIDE TRACK
ABOUT HYBRIDS

Hybrids are crosses between different species of grapevine. In wine, these are typically bred to marry the aesthetic advantages of vinifera with the durability of another species. Vinifera is responsible for the world's finest wines, but as a species it is sensitive to cold, drought and disease. The inclusion of even a minor percentage of non-vinifera DNA can strengthen it considerably, but the wine intelligentsia is often quick to dismiss the resulting wine's flavour.

Hybrids have a diminished reputation in wine, but climate change is forcing a re-examination of that position. In Europe, they are not allowed to be included in 'quality' or appellated wines, but the New World is considerably more open. The curious wine drinker will find interesting examples from the United States, especially outside of the classic wine producing states of California, Oregon and Washington.

DECODING TERMS:
ORGANIC, BIODYNAMIC, SUSTAINABLE AND REGENERATIVE

I know a shocking number of people who spend a fortune on organic groceries, but when it comes to wine will happily chug the cheapest, most industrially made bottle without a second thought. I've always wondered at this behaviour. My recent thinking is that some people see wine as just another beverage rather than an agricultural product. They don't register that wine, too, is farmed.

The consumer who does care how their drinks are made is a bit disadvantaged when it comes to wine. The landscape is fragmented, opaque and occasionally contradictory. Sometimes it feels as if there aren't enough certifications out there, and other times it feels as if there are too many. For example, there are at least three different organizations that certify if a vineyard is farmed biodynamically (Demeter, Respekt and Biodyvin) but none that can tell me if the processes put an undue strain on water reserves or how the farmworkers are treated.

The lack of visibility into farming practices is compounded by the fact that many growers eschew certification, often because it is costly and time-consuming. Still others pick and choose from different schools of thought, and therefore don't fit neatly into the categories below. There's a winemaker I know who farms organically but is disqualified from certification since they occasionally employ a synthetic fungicide (their site is particularly mildew-prone). That same person also incorporates a handful of biodynamic practices. Looking at the label, a consumer would never know any of the above. This winery is farming in what they believe is the most holistic way for their location, but there is no certification for 'doing their best' or 'better than most'.

Having said that, though the existing certifications are narrow, they do provide a helpful shortcut for concerned shoppers. Anyone wanting to know more about the specific practices of an uncertified wine will have to ask either their merchant or sommelier for help.

Below is a guide to some of the major movements in conscientious farming, as well as definitions of key terms.

Conventional viticulture

Before we can discuss alternatives, we need to define conventional viticulture. What it is, what it entails and why some farmers are moving away from it.

First of all, conventional viticulture isn't necessarily evil or bad. It is called 'conventional' merely because it is the most widespread. This style of farming tends to rely on synthetic pesticides to eradicate pests, synthetic fungicides to fight mildew and other diseases, and synthetic herbicides to remove pesky weeds from under the vines. In some places, conventional farming might also involve regular ploughing and a reliance on irrigation. Note my use of the words 'some' and 'tends'; there is no official conventional farming rulebook, so practices vary widely.

Conventional viticulture is often the cheapest and easiest way to farm, especially where labour is scarce. But cost-saving is not always the motivation for farming in this way. While you can be assured that very inexpensive wines are farmed conventionally, you cannot assume that expensive wines are farmed more responsibly. There are many pricey and renowned wines that rely on synthetic sprays, mineral fertilizers, regular ploughing and water by the truckload.

Organic

Organic farming can appear very similar to conventional farming, with the primary difference being that organics does not allow the use of synthetic chemical inputs and compost is preferred to mineral fertilizers. Because organic sprays tend to be less effective, they may need to be applied more often, which means more tractor passes. This is often criticized as increasing both the carbon footprint and soil compaction of organically farmed sites.

Note that, at least in the United States, there is a distinction between a 'wine made from organic grapes' and an 'organic wine'. The most significant restriction pertains to sulphur usage (*see* page 207).

Biodynamic

I get a *lot* of questions about biodynamics. People seem mystified – and sometimes amused – at what can appear to be a very arcane and bizarre style of farming. Burying a cow horn full of manure, digging it up several months later and using it to make a tea, then spraying that tea on the vines, feels as baroque and supernatural as a witch's spell. But is it really so very different to taking a yoga class, drinking some chamomile and checking your horoscope? Modern life isn't always so modern upon examination.

The collective practices known as Biodynamics stem from a series of lectures delivered by the supremely problematic Rudolph Steiner in 1924. This was a moment in history where, several decades after the Industrial Revolution, humanity had settled into a comfortable reliance on monoculture and agrochemical farming. Though farmers were producing more food than ever, it was arguably less nutritionally dense, and the processes creating that bounty were unsustainable. The wholesale eradication of a given insect, for instance, might allow the entry of a worse bug, which would then require an even stronger pesticide. And so on and so forth until the whole system crashes.

Biodynamics encourages the grower to consider the total health of the vineyard, rather than focus on specific issues. The idea being that a robust and balanced ecosystem will have greater natural immunity to a range of problems. Biodynamics preaches biodiversity – the inclusion of other plant and animal life among the vines – but this is not enforced. Its practices often involve herbs and animals, and some are timed according to celestial movements. The spiritual intention of the farmer is also emphasized.

Many of the greatest wines in the world are farmed Biodynamically or utilize at least some of its methods. Cynics sometimes contend that this has less to do with Biodynamics itself than the fact that its practitioners tend to spend considerable time in the vineyard.

Note *A Biodynamic vineyard is organic by default.*

Regenerative
Regenerative farming is a relatively new initiative in vine growing. Here, the focus is on soil health, rebuilding topsoil and carbon sequestration. Ploughing is highly discouraged, and the use of cover crops and animal fertilizers is recommended.

Sustainable
Sustainable viticulture casts a wide net. Though in principle it communicates to the consumer a higher-than-average farming standard, critics complain that it allows too many unsavoury practices and that

bad actors can use the term for 'green-washing'. Having said that, there are a number of mostly regional (as opposed to national) initiatives worth investigating. Some of the more comprehensive include winery practices, social initiatives and carbon footprint analyses.

Dry-farming

A dry-farmed vineyard is farmed without irrigation; the vines must capture all their water from precipitation or by accessing underground sources. Sometimes, a dry-farmed vineyard will be irrigated for the first handful of years after planting, so the baby vines have an opportunity to get established.

Permaculture

Permaculture is a design-forward system that seeks to minimize effort, inputs and waste. It is similar to Biodynamics in its natural, holistic approach but is less dogmatic in practice.

Biodiversity

Modern farming is all about isolating products: a field full of only corn, a barn full of only cows. This may seem like the most efficient and cost-effective way to farm, but such conditions invite disease which then require the use of antibiotics, chemical sprays or even genetically modified organisms. Proponents of biodiversity advocate a movement away from monoculture through the integration of different animals and plants.

Integrated Pest Management (IPM)

IPM was a pre-cursor to the modern sustainability movement and seeks to avoid the overuse of pesticides through the harnessing of natural advantages. Common practices include the introduction of predators to tamp down the population of a troublesome pest and the use of pheromones to interrupt insect mating cycles. The latter is known colloquially as 'sexual confusion'.

ON LABOUR

Labour is a difficult point of conversation in wine, and the place where the industry needs the most reform. Much of the complication stems from the fact that harvest requires a sudden influx of manpower, and the timing is similar for all producers in a given region. As a result of this acute need, the common practice has become to import large forces of migrant labour that travel to the area either for the growing season (ie, summer) or just for harvest.

The temporary nature of this employment sometimes means that workers are not provided with adequate insurance, training or housing. This system offers cost-savings to the wineries but can be exploitative to workers. It draws upon unfavourable economic conditions that encourage workers to leave their home countries in pursuit of more profitable international work, sometimes without the legal protection of official channels. In the United States, citizens aren't even necessarily safe, as agricultural workers can be disenfranchised relative to other fields. Labour shortages in many wine regions are of growing concern, and solutions seem difficult to come by. Globally, the situation can be described as unstable at best.

Happily, there is a rising awareness of labour dynamics in the wine industry, though it is by no means a mainstream concern. As a consumer, the best thing you can do to ask questions. Ask your retailer or sommelier about the labour practices of a given winery. They very well may not know the answers, but it will hopefully inspire them to enquire of the distributors, importers or even the producers themselves. Are the farmworkers well compensated? Are they offered insurance and other protections? Training and education? Or, best of all, are they retained as year-round employees?

Who knows – a few uncomfortable questions may provide the butterfly effect that changes things for the better.

There are specific times of year when the need for labour becomes acute. Harvest is one such time, and the pruning season, at the tail end of winter, is another.

9

Take the List!

I hate the date dynamic wherein someone sits in polite silence while their companion makes all the decisions. This is probably because I've been on the wrong side of it for too long. Even when I'm the most knowledgeable person in the group, my gender ensures that I'm rarely handed the wine list. And let's not talk about the bill!

I wish restaurants would stop making assumptions about who is taking the lead in these circumstances. (Some restaurants, that is – I've had lovely experiences in many places.) Handing the wine list to one person at a table reinforces the idea that wine belongs to some and not others. And consistently defaulting to the oldest male at the table sends a powerful message. This is why I'm always telling people to *take the list*. Even if you are only just beginning to learn about wine. Especially if you are not the person to whom it would normally be given.

I've spent the last 200 or so pages discussing wine's aesthetic value and detailing all the ways it can improve your life. But now I'd like to make a more capitalistic appeal: a working knowledge of wine is not just good for the soul; it can offer material benefits as well. Here, I am going to tell you some stories of wine empowerment.

WINE IS FOR EVERYONE

When I worked as a sommelier in New York, a nervous businessman in his 30s wandered into the restaurant before opening. He was hosting a big client dinner that night and wanted help selecting a bottle. He knew a little bit about wine, but our list was several inches thick and overwhelming. We talked about his budget and what he knew about his clients' preferences and zeroed in on a few suggestions. I then walked him through what would pair best with the wines and armed him with some charming stories about the producers.

That night, in front of his clients, we pretended to meet for the first time, and I told the table how impressed I was with his selections. The following afternoon a bouquet of flowers was waiting on my desk. Our bit of theatre had won him the contract.

I'm under no illusion that the wine selections alone sealed the deal; surely a solid foundation had already been laid. But I do believe that sometimes seemingly small advantages can tip the scales in our favour. Wine can be one such advantage, and the pursuit of wine knowledge can unlock a surprising number of other skills, as well.

WINE IS THE NEW GOLF

Networking is key to any career, whether you're a lawyer, a plumber or a high school teacher. And a big part of successful networking is making a personal connection; that's how you move yourself from background to front of mind. In the rarified air of business, finance and law, the classic trope is deals are struck on the golf course. Why? Golfing gets people outside, where they can relax, slow down and discuss something other than work.

Wine is also a great way to form connections away from the office. Plus, it can be enjoyed year-round and requires neither athletic proficiency nor an affinity for plaid. In researching this section, I spoke to several professionals about the intersection of wine and work. Many of them began the conversation by saying 'I don't golf', or 'I don't ski', or 'I don't know about watches' and then went on to detail how wine saved them from these deficits and helped them form beneficial business connections. Sometimes their wine knowledge served to bridge a daunting socioeconomic gap, other times it was the way into the secretly tender heart of a difficult client.

One woman I chatted to linked the 'multidisciplinary nature of wine knowledge' to her ability 'to connect with a wide range of people, personally and professionally'. Another extolled wine's ability to 'open doors to other topics like travel and food, farming and even engineering'. And a young female investment banker commented that she was able to use wine at work dinners as a way to break the ice, to make the conversation lighter and to form meaningful bonds. 'The wine was something in common that the whole table talked about.'

This idea that relationships are formed or strengthened through the sharing of a meal is hardly radical. But this is more often discussed in the context of friends and family, not co-workers. And yet I recently learned of an MBA professor who takes his students to wine country as part of their curriculum. He believes that true negotiations occur not in the boardroom but over the dinner table and encourages the pursuit of wine knowledge as both a legitimate business strategy and pathway for career advancement.

For one woman, learning about wine began as a way to relate to her colleagues, but ultimately led to a career change. 'When I was working in tech during the first dot-com wave, I worked in an incubator and so had to have dinner with venture capital guys all the time. They were all old white men with whom I had nothing in common.' A friend suggested she take a wine class as a way to cultivate a shared interest. 'I took some classes, and not only did it give me a way to connect, but it also blew my mind open and set me on the wine path.'

Speaking of professional makeovers, one man's interest in wine led to an unexpected opportunity. 'I was looking for a career change five years ago, from home improvement retail… I posted in the *Wine Spectator* forums a lot and met a guy who was selling wine. We began hanging out and he introduced me to a lot of other people. A bunch were in the biotech/pharma industry.' Fast-forward through some networking and helpful resume prep, and he now works as a buyer for a biotech company.

PASSION AS PASSPORT

Beyond networking, a certain degree of wine expertise can help a person stand out from the crowd. It might even fast-track their career in terms of gaining key invitations and opportunities.

One interviewee recounted: 'As an academic philosopher, knowing how to read a wine list and infer what kind of wine a visiting international researcher/speaker/professor would like, got me invited regularly to the dinners celebrating visiting researchers, and usually seated beside them as well.' Because of wine, this scholar was able to meet and form connections with some of the world's most respected minds at a relatively early career stage.

Another young professional was offered a job when someone overheard her talking about wine in a coffee shop. A handful of tech people were starting a wine app and needed someone with wine knowledge on their team. She quickly found herself at parties with some of the biggest names in business. Whenever she felt in over her head, she steered the conversation back to wine and regained common ground. A budding filmmaker employed a similar strategy. 'When I was young and interested in film, I'd often mention wine

early on. Then me as a 25-year-old had a way to communicate with a successful person in their 50s because we could connect over a common language with wine,' he admitted, adding: 'It got me dinners and friendships and meetings I'd never have got otherwise.'

One of my favourite stories surrounding the intersection of wine and film involves a famous director and a dolly-operator. The film shoot happened to be taking place in British Columbia, and the wine-loving dolly-operator was something of a local expert. When he overheard the director talking about wine, he decided to gift him a bottle. The director loved the selection so much, he asked the dolly-operator for more wine advice, a transactional exchange that blossomed into a personal connection. Now, any time the director is filming in BC, he insists the dolly-operator is on his crew. 'I can't stress enough how not normal this friendship is,' his wife confessed, 'and it's all thanks to wine and wine knowledge.'

During the course of my interviews, many claimed that having some wine experience on their resume gave their application an edge, especially if they were applying within non-wine-related industries. According to one: 'When applying for my first law jobs I would say 75 percent of lead-off interview questions were about wine because my resume noted I ran the law school wine tasting club. Which meant the ice was broken, the interviews flowed more easily, and ultimately were more successful.' Another recalled that, at the end of his first post-MBA internship, his company arranged a team-building exercise at a local wine bar. Coming from a service background, he nailed the blind tasting, which seemed to impress his bosses. Shortly thereafter, he was offered a permanent position.

Sometimes it's not just wine knowledge in general, but familiarity with specific bottles that offers the advantage. During a business dinner with vendors, one attendee grabbed the wine list and ordered a rare Spanish rosé for the table. A particularly efficient salesman took a photo of the bottle and uploaded it to his expense tracker as per his reporting requirements. Shortly thereafter, the salesman's phone rang. It was the company's CFO. Because it was after 10 pm, he was nervous, and walked around a corner to take the call. 'Seconds later he's back with his hand over the phone saying, "he wants to talk to you!". Turns out the CFO was a huge wine nerd, too.'

A different salesman used both his wine knowledge and bargain-hunting skills to curry favour within his company. 'I studied wine in order to make the most of my expense budget,' he recalls, and was especially fond of second labels from famous houses. 'Back in 1999, the Berry Bros & Rudd website would let you click on the name of a wine, and it would pronounce it for you, so I could go into a client situation not looking like a moron.' His knack for finding excellent wines for reasonable sums soon impressed the finance team. 'I would get invited to steakhouse dinners with clients to navigate the wine list, so they weren't just buying the most expensive thing… It was cheaper just to pay for my steak.'

SOCIAL CURRENCY

Both within the boardroom and without, wine knowledge can elevate someone's social standing. It might even help combat negative stereotypes. For some black, indigenous people and people of colour, as well as members of the LGBTQ+ community, it can prove useful when facing discrimination.

As one entrepreneur put it, 'of course there are a lot of assumptions I'm making in the way I've felt I've been perceived as a young female person of colour, but I have on numerous occasions felt I've been taken more seriously intellectually once I've demonstrated an ability to speak intelligently on a topic on which the other person (usually older… and almost always male) has presumed themselves to be the authority on.'

Another woman uses her wine knowledge as a kind of armour. 'I find that being able to speak about wine is a bit of a shield for myself as a BIPOC woman. When I visit wine country, or even order in restaurants, it's a way to indicate that I'm not just a tourist (not that I think there's anything wrong with tourists), speak fluent English and that I am worthy of the same service as someone Western.'

Proving your wine chops can even be important inside the industry, as an accomplished winemaker recounted: 'I have countless memories of straight men being uncomfortable in my presence because of me being gay. No doubt about it. I always had to be the one breaking the ice and showing my knowledge.'

SOFT SKILLS

Studying wine can do more than add to your bottom line and forge connections between people; it can also broaden both your skill-sets and horizons in unexpected ways.

Consider the following disparate tales:

- A Chief Technology Officer I spoke to encourages wine studies for 'engineering types' because they tend to be overly linear thinkers. 'Wine takes something that is technical but also analytical and covers sensory domains. Then that is communicated via language, writing and storytelling. This is a very transferable set of skills!'

- A gentleman claimed his pursuit of wine knowledge eased his return to civilian life. 'It's certainly become clearer that the soft skills are just as important as the hard facts [in wine]. It's really has been a key part in my transition out of the military.'
- A Korean woman felt the conversation shifting to Italian wine swung her US citizenship interview in her favour.
- And another gentleman leveraged his passion for wine to overcome a resistance to studying that was so extreme, he used to break out in hives.

Wine can also be a source of inner power. 'In my early days of wine knowledge,' one woman confessed, 'it gave me the confidence to solo travel or sit at a restaurant on my own.' Another found that, after decades working in IT, wine opened unforeseen avenues of intellectual pursuit. 'I never expected that through my 50s and into my 60s, I'd become extremely interested in farming, geology, biology, chemistry, biodiversity, sustainability, business, oenology and, yes, even geography.' And a social worker in Oregon uses wine knowledge to bolster her sense of self-worth. 'Sometimes I feel less intellectually sharp among peers or even just than my younger self. So when I have those moments of self-doubt, I remind myself that I passed [a wine exam] with distinction! This might seem silly but I'm proud of that and the work it took.'

WINE AS PERSONALITY QUIZ

The majority of people I spoke with used wine to demonstrate something about themselves. But a handful used wine knowledge to gain insight into others.

One particularly savvy female investment banker saw wine as a way to connect with her predominately male clients, but quickly discovered a link between a person's taste in wine and their professional habits. Do they drink only blue-chip wines? Are they passionate about organics? Enjoy the thrill of a new discovery? Prefer something cheap and cheerful? Drink exclusively natural wine? By navigating her client's wine preferences, she was able to intuit their financial and business needs with remarkable accuracy.

A former Bay Area sommelier has created a successful business using wine to mine for insightful information that can be leveraged to close deals. Her company specializes in hosting wine tastings, both in person and virtual, for the tech sector. During the course of an event, she will tell stories and ask questions, drawing personal information out of what is often a somewhat reticent demographic. She makes note of favourite producers, landmark vintages (weddings, births of children), significant travel memories, and turns them into personalized gifts for the attendees. A couple of years in, her unique services have generated millions of dollars in revenue for her clients.

The decision whether or not to do business with someone can be a significant consideration. Which is why one health care investment executive uses wine as a way to evaluate potential business partners. 'How someone handles themself at a dinner table is absolutely revealing about their real personality, so it's a critical element when in a business relationship.' Though perfectly capable of ordering the wine herself, she allows others to do it as a kind of mini-audition. 'From the way that someone orders, I can tell not just how much they know, but how comfortable they are in their own skin, and how inclusive and inquisitive they are.' This then guides the nature of their business relationship going forwards.

For herself, the more comfortable she has become with wine, the less she feels compelled to know everything. 'Looking at a wine list, it's less about knowing all the vintages, producers and vineyards,' she explained. 'And more about knowing how to ask the right questions of the right people in order to get the desired outcome.'

And that, she believes, is a life skill with a value that extends far beyond wine, into the professional realm.

THE FINISH

If you've come this far, I thank you. I know it is the fate of many wine books to gather dust in a forgotten corner – I have piles of them myself. But I sincerely hope you've enjoyed what you've read in this one. These pages are the result of decades spent toiling and tasting my way through the various corners of the wine industry; time that I consider well-spent and rich with lessons.

In writing this book, I wanted to entertain you, to make you think, and inspire you to learn more. But most of all, I wanted to be of service. This may be my sommelier background speaking, but it's true. When I close my eyes and image this book out in the world, it is dog-eared, wine-stained and heavy with underlining.

Please use this book as a stepping stone to a greater appreciation of wine. Or as a literal stepping stone if it will help you reach that top shelf bottle.

I sincerely believe that learning about wine will improve your life. Not only can it slow down time, strengthen friendships and unlock a hidden world of flavour, but it might even forge business alliances, buttress your confidence and improve your financial status. This is a lot to promise! And there's only one way to find out if wine makes good in the end.

As I said in the beginning, the most important things to remember are to stay curious and stay thirsty. So go forth! Read, drink, travel, take notes, break bread and break corks.

And don't forget to take the list.

> **Please use this book as a stepping stone to a greater appreciation of wine. Or as a literal stepping stone if it will help you reach that top shelf bottle.**

Further Reading

The following is very far from a complete list of worthy wine books. These simply represent the tomes I have reached for the most during the course of my career.

General information

Secrets of the Sommeliers – Rajat Parr and Jordan Mackay; Ten Speed Press (2010)

The Oxford Companion to Wine – Jancis Robinson MW; OUP (2023)

The Wine Bible – Karen MacNeil; Workman (2022)

The World Atlas of Wine – Hugh Johnson and Jancis Robinson MW; Mitchell Beazley (2019)

The World in a Wine Glass – Ray Isle; Scribner (2023)

Windows on the World Complete Wine Course – Kevin Zraly; Sterling (2016)

Speciality Topics

Appellation Napa Valley – Richard Mendelson; Val de Grace (2016)

Barolo MGA – Alessandro Masnaghetti; Giunti Editore (2015)

Burgundy Vintages – Allen Meadows and Douglas E Barzelay; Burghound Books (2018)

Champagne – Peter Liem; Mitchell Beazley (2017)

Cote D'Or – Clive Coates MW; UCP (1997)

Decantations – Frank Prial; St Martin's Griffin (2002)

Drinking with the Valkyries – Andrew Jefford; AdVL (2022)

Inside Bordeaux – Jane Anson; BB&R Press (2020)

Inside Burgundy – Jasper Morris; BB&R Press (2010)

Native Wine Grapes of Italy – Ian D'Agata; UCP (2014)

On Bordeaux – Académie du Vin Library (AdVL) (2020)

On Burgundy – Académie du Vin Library (2023)

On California – Académie du Vin Library (2021)

On Champagne – Académie du Vin Library (2022)

Oz Clarke's Story of Wine – Oz Clarke; Pavilion Books (2023)

Sherry, Manzanilla and Montilla – Peter Liem; Manutius (2012)

The Dirty Guide to Wine – Alice Feiring with Pascaline Lepeltier; Countryman Press (2017)

The New California – Jon Bonné; Ten Speed Press (2013)

The New France – Andrew Jefford; Mitchell Beazley (2002)

The New Spain – John Radford; Mitchell Beazley (2004)

The Pearl of the Côte – Allen Meadows; Burghound Books (2010)

The Taste of Wine – Emile Peynaud; Little, Brown (1987)

The Wines of the Rhône Valley – Robert M Parker; Simon & Schuster (1997)

Vintage Timecharts – Jancis Robinson MW; Grove Press (2018)

Vintage Wine – Michael Broadbent; Little, Brown (2002)

Voodoo Vintners – Katherine Cole; Oregon State University Press (2011)

Wine Science

Flawless – Jamie Goode; University of California Press (UCP) (Berkeley) 2018

Neurogastronomy – Gordon M Shepherd; Columbia University Press (2013)

The New Viticulture – Jamie Goode; Flavour Press (2023)

The Science of Wine – Jamie Goode; UCP (2020)

The Winemaker's Dance – Jonathan Swinchatt and David G Howell; UCP (2004)

Understanding Wine Technology – David Bird MW; DBQA Publishing (2010)

Wine Grapes – Jancis Robinson MW, Julia Harding MW and José Vouillamoz; Allen Lane (2012).

Wine History

French Wine, A History – Rod Philips; UCP (2016)

Napa Wine – Charles Sullivan; Wine Appreciation Guild (2008)

The Story of Wine – Hugh Johnson; AdVL (2020)

Wine Tasting – Michael Broadbent; AdVL (2019)

Wine & War – Don and Petie Kladstrup; Hodder (2002)

Human Interest

Adventures On the Wine Route – Kermit Lynch; Farrar, Straus and Giroux (2019)

How to Love Wine – Eric Asimov; William Morrow (2012)

Judgment of Paris – George M Taber; Scribner (2006)

Love by the Glass – Dorothy J Gaiter and John Brecher; Random House (2003)

Vignette – Jane Lopes; Quadrille (2019)

Vineyard Tales – Gerald Asher; Chronicle Books (2000)

Grape Varieties

Arranged from light white to deep, dark red, this chart is a simple guide to the weight of wine you can expect from each grape. But remember, bottles vary. Every wine will differ depending on its region, producer, vintage and bottle age.

WHITE

Trebbiano – For the most part, wines bearing this name are fresh, crisp and fruity and meant for drinking young. However, there are some truly profound examples such as a handful of mineral-laced beauties from Abruzzo (Italy).

Aligoté – Native to Burgundy, wines from this grape are bright, fruity, and prone to neutrality, though can rise to the occasion when a quality producer treats them with tender loving care.

Albariño – Crisp, aromatic, and slightly salty white from Portugal and northwest Spain. Due to its ability to tolerate drought and heat, yet produce a wine of lively acidity, Albariño is beginning to crop up in a wide range of unexpected regions, worldwide.

Sylvaner – An underrated variety whose neutral everyday presence can occasionally give way to dense, peachy brilliance if treated with care and planted in top sites. This most often happens in Alsace where it is considered a noble variety.

Assyrtiko – Fresh, crisp, full of citrus and bergamot minerality and honeyed complex textures; most at home on the Greek island of Santorini but increasingly popular around the world.

Torrontés – Argentina's signature white grape, popular for its fresh aromatic wines with moderate acidity and smooth, peachy mouthfeel.

Pinot Blanc – Delightful for its pear, floral and pink grapefruit aromas and smooth gentle peachiness on the palate: a great match for spicy foods. Most at home in Germany and Alsace; occasionally thrilling in Champagne.

Pinot Grigio/Gris – Popular pinkish grape making fresh, light wines that can vary from light and spritzy (Northern Italy) to rich, oily and lightly tropical (Alsace, New Zealand).

Sauvignon Blanc – Popular white grape beloved for its crisp, aromatic, unoaked character. Though globally planted, certain regions have become known for distinctive styles, from steely Sancerre to broad Bordeaux to grassy Marlborough and tropical Napa Valley. Excellent in dessert form, eg Sauternes.

Furmint – High-acidity Central European variety with superb ageing potential. Excels in Hungary where it is the qualitative leader in the blends that compose that country's famous Tokaji dessert wines. Fermented on its own, and to dryness, the wine is steely, lime-kissed, and fine.

Riesling – Cool-climate, slow-ripening grape with highly distinctive apple, honey and petrol aromas and incredible ageing potential. Many consider it to be among the finest white grapes of the world. Riesling excels across the full spectrum of sweet to dry; a characteristic that is both a blessing and a curse, as some consumers find this variability confusing.

Ribolla Gialla – A rather tannic variety, Ribolla Gialla makes some deeply layered, slightly floral, age-worthy white wines. It is also a popular variety for skin contact ('orange') wines.

Grüner Veltliner – Loved in Austria for its complex honeyed wines with brisk acidity, GV can develop stunning complexity with age and is increasingly popular for its matchability with all manner of foods.

Gewurztraminer – This unmistakable French grape, from Alsace, gives rounded, full-bodied, golden wines with low acidity and distinctive lychee and rose petal aromas. Quality examples can also be found in North Italy, Oregon and the Finger Lakes (NY State).

Chenin Blanc – Crisp, appley, acidic wines that can vary from bone-dry to lusciously sweet. Best known in the Loire Valley but historically important in South Africa and California. Can be quite age-worthy.

Chardonnay – This versatile grape can range from crisp, flinty and delicate (Chablis) to richly honeyed and tropical (oak-aged California) to bright and bubbly (champagne). Can develop beautifully with age.

Semillon – Though most often seen in a blend with Sauvignon Blanc, where it contributes a waxy, honeyed richness, Semillon is also highly regarded for serious, dry, long-ageing whites in Australia.

Roussanne – Often blended with Marsanne or other Rhône whites; found across much of Southern France. Produces heady, floral wines that are substantial yet rarely heavy, and have a refined acidity. The best age well, taking on a rich honeyed tone.

RED

Barbera – Fiesty, vibrant, cherry-bombs. Barbera is an important grape in Piemonte, where it can produce wines that range from charming to serious. Its ability to retain a sometimes startlingly high acidity in spite of heat has also made it an important factor in parts of California, specifically the Sierra Foothills.

Gamay – Famous for its light-bodied fruity wines that are drunk young ('Beaujolais Nouveau'), Gamay can make for serious, intricate and profound wines when grown on top sites.

Dolcetto – A cheerful grape with bouncy, floral aromatics and surprisingly dark hue. Mostly seen in the Piemonte region of Italy where examples range from charming fruit-bombs to clove-laden beauties.

Pinot Noir – Hailing from Burgundy, France, where it makes lingeringly elegant red wines full of wild cherry and earthy finesse. Never heavy or dark. Known for its unique ability to communicate terroir.

Grenache – Vibrant, juicy (strawberry and plum) and smooth, as well as generally light in hue. Grenache is most widely seen in the South of France and across Spain, where it is known as Garnacha. Increasingly popular in the New World, especially the Americas.

Merlot – Celebrated for its soft red cherry and plum fruit (less austere and concentrated than its partner Cabernet Sauvignon), Merlot is well-known as a Bordeaux blend component but has huge popularity right across the wine world.

Cabernet Franc – Popular French variety known for its savoury palate and herbal aromatic lift. In the Loire Valley it excels as a single varietal wine, while in Bordeaux it is most commonly found in a blend. Growing in importance in the Super Tuscan reds of Bolgheri, Italy as well as Napa Valley.

Sangiovese – Darling of Italy, and capable of a broad qualitative range. On the one hand is a sea of easy fruity quaffers. On the other is a growing number of profoundly age-worthy and stately reds of great depth and exceptional finesse.

Zinfandel – California's signature grape (despite its Croatian origin) that produces large bunches of grapes that ripen at different rates, often to the consternation of the grower. Though it is best known for off-dry, fruity rosé and jammy, high alcohol reds, if treated correctly it can yield wonderfully complex, layered and vibrant wines.

Malbec – French grape now highly successful in Argentina for its full-bodied wines, deep in colour with blackberry-plum fruit, rich tannins and a hint of tobacco leaf.

Syrah/Shiraz – A versatile grape whose stylistic expression ranges from dark, meaty and savoury in many Australian Shirazes, to peppery and floral in the Northern Rhône, to polished and richly-berried in much of Caliornia.

Tempranillo – A key component of Rioja in Spain where it shows black cherry and tobacco-leaf flavours and a deep affinity with oak, ageing magnificently in barrel. Also making a home for itself in Portugal, Washington, Oregon, California and Australia's Adelaide Hills.

Nebbiolo – Proud producer of Northern Italy's most prestigious wines, Barolo and Barbaresco, this high-acid, tannic, rose-and-tar grape undergoes a magical transformation with age that's hard to replicate elsewhere in the world.

Cabernet Sauvignon – Adored for its firm blackcurrant fruitiness that can develop tantalizing complexity with age in barrel and bottle. Bordeaux is its spiritual and historic home but world-class examples can be found around the globe, especially in Napa Valley (California), Maipo Valley (Chile), and Coonawarra (Australia).

Petite Sirah – Most at home in California, where it makes wines of deep colour, edgy tannins and chewy richness, with plenty of blackcurrant power. Can age surprisingly well.

Aglianico – One of the great red grapes of Italy, highly tannic, powerfully acidic, deeply concentrated, and in need of several years ageing before you approach it.

Xinomavro – Dark, tannic, and capable of great age, this fairly obscure variety is native to Northern mainland Greece, where it thrives in Naoussa.

Index

Page numbers in *italic* refer to the illustrations

Commissioned photography:
© 2024 by Emma K Creative /emmakcreative.com p8, p11,
p18, p26, p38, p39, p48, p68, p86, p102, p106 (*left, centre*),
p107, p109, p119, p154

Other photography:
© Scott Brenner p101, p105, p108, p111, p127, p129, p132,
p141 (*top*), p163, p170, p181, p199 (*bottom*), p203, p214 (*top*),
p217 (*top left*); p237, p238, p241

p20 Adobe Stock; p62 Adobe Stock; p67 Adobe Stock;
p75 Adobe Stock; p81 AdVL Lucy Pope; p89 Adobe Stock;
p91 Adobe Stock; p106 (*right*) Shutterstock; p112 Adobe Stock;
p141 (*centre, bottom*) AdVL Lucy Pope; p145 AdVL Lucy Pope;
p162 Adobe Stock; p169 Adobe Stock; p175 Adobe Stock;
p211 Adobe Stock; p212 Adobe Stock; p214 (*centre*) Shutterstock,
(*bottom*) Adobe Stock; p217 (*top right*) Adobe Stock,
(*bottom left, right*) AdVL; p227 Adobe Stock

The publishers have made every effort to trace the copyright
holders of the text and images reproduced in this book. If,
however, you believe that any work has been incorrectly credited
or used without permission, please contact us immediately and
we will endeavour to rectify the situation.

Acknowledgments

A number of people helped me through the process of writing *Wine Confident*, but the simple truth is that the book would not exist today without the kind words of Elaine Chukan Brown. There is a maxim floating in the more inspirational currents of the internet that goes something like, 'surround yourself with people who would speak your name in a room full of opportunity'. That is exactly what Elaine did. As the former US executive editor for JancisRobinson.com and current columnist for *Decanter*, Elaine is deeply imbedded in the British wine writing scene. And when the Académie du Vin Library began commissioning authors for its *On California* anthology in 2019, Elaine suggested the editor contact me. The result was a well-received chapter entitled 'The Boffins, from Hilgard to Amerine' and, ultimately, this book.

Elaine – inasmuch as we have 'beats', ours overlap considerably. And yet instead of competing, we continually choose to celebrate each other. Thank you for speaking my name. I am forever in your debt.

Heartfelt thanks are also owed to Hermione Ireland, the managing director of Académie du Vin Library, AdVL's talented designers Tim Foster and James Pople, Adam Lechmere, and editorial director Susan Keevil. Especially Susan, for her endless patience, kindness, and for encouraging me to write in my natural voice. Thank you for letting me tell my goofy stories and for believing that they might be of some value. Thank you, also, for your red pen. I hope that one day you can forgive my blatant disregard for accepted comma usage.

Sincere thanks are also owed to Bill Harlan, who trusted me to write this book while under his full-time employ. Your love of the written word seems to run as deep as your love of wine, and it's one of the many things about you that I admire. This is probably a good moment to state that the views espoused in this publication are completely my own, and do not necessarily reflect the beliefs of the greater Harlan family of wine. And gratitude goes to my greater work families at Meadowood and The Napa Valley Reserve, for their kind and unwavering support.

Alisha Sommer, Stacy Ladenburger, Jonny Miles, 'Petruski', June Rodil MS and Lynn Elliott deserve eternal thanks for agreeing to be early readers of this work... Their commentary, not to mention their love and moral support, proved essential. Stevie Stacionis was my rock, bestowing critical feedback and the occasional kick in the pants, Francis Percival acted as both counsellor and British ambassador to this project. Jess Mennella was one part stage mom and two parts scent consultant. Ema Koeda withstood many questions. Dr Jamie Goode, Jenn Angelosante and Alexandra Cubbage provided critical fact-checking services. Patrick Cappiello reviewed the restaurant and natural wine bits. And Karen MacNeil, my forever-inspiration and pillar of support, cheered me on as always.

I would also like to thank my current and former colleagues in wine education – Chris Tanghe MS, Bryce Wiatrak and Sarah Bray – for making me a better communicator through their examples. Extra gratitude is owed to Sarah Bray, with whom I've workshopped some of the concepts outlaid in this book during our time teaching together. You deserve all the gold stars. And a heaping helping of good will, with a pink gorilla on top, goes to Josh Nadel MS, who always keeps his doors open.

On the flipside, I'd also like to thank my various clients and students who have trusted me with their instruction over the years. Thank you for your honesty, your curiosity and your vulnerability. It was your questions, more than anything else, that guided the shape of this book.

It was the thrill of a lifetime to have the preposterously talented Emma Kruch contribute photography for this book. And thank you, also, to my unpaid models: Christopher Gaither MS and his daughters Edith Louisa Fineman and Josephine Mae Gaither, Stevie Stacionis, Josiah and Foxen Baldivino, Alisha and Michael Sommer, Elaine Chukan Brown, Amy Yang, Michael Hirby and Schatzi Throckmorton. Thank you for your faces, bodies, hands and beautiful smiles. I'm sorry that I couldn't find the forks. And thank you to my husband for providing much of the balance of the photography.

Finally, I want to thank my family. To my mother Diane and sister Robin – thank you for your infinite love and support. All I ever want is to make you proud. Thank you to Sophi Jacobs, my best friend of 25 years, for lovingly calling out my pretentions (that wine really was corked, though).

Ziggy – thank you for sharing your mommy with this project. I promise that life going forward will be nothing but pony rides and minigolf. And to my dear husband, Scott: thank you for picking up the slack, for navigating my meltdowns, and for your emphatic belief in my abilities. I promise that life going forward will be nothing but family walks and champagne on the back deck.